LIVING A MORE INTENTIONAL LIFE

**(A fable to help individuals, couples, and
teams build more meaningful relationships)**

**The Spiritual Patterns and Principles
Five Building Blocks to help you develop the
skills to reach your full God-given potential!**

BY

CARY MASSEY

*To: Derrick & Iris
God Bless*

CHAPTER 1

THE ENCOUNTER

Every day at 6 a.m. Cole Gastone woke up with the same five words nagging at him. They had been rattling around in his head for quite some time now. It didn't matter that he had what most people considered to be a wonderful life. As he prepared for work, his daily routine was filled with those five words. They kept eating at him, day in and day out. How could a forty-three-year-old successful realtor have these kinds of thoughts? He has a beautiful wife and two adorable kids. They live in a home that is the envy of most couples. But still, he couldn't shake those five nagging words.

He and Alisha have been married for thirteen years. The first few years were great. It felt like a marriage made in heaven. Now, after some "settling in," they just seem to be married. It's not that Cole is unhappy, it's just that it doesn't feel like he thought happy was supposed to feel. The daily routine is beginning to get to him. He gets up, goes to work, comes home, eats dinner, and watches TV, day after day. That seems to be the origin of the five nagging words, "**Is that all there is?**"

When he left the insurance business to venture out and make his mark on the world, he didn't give a thought to that persistent question that has plagued man since the beginning of time. Now, even though he, seemingly, has it all he just can't keep those five words from pressing down on him. They seem to be sucking the life out of him.

But today will not be consumed by those nagging thoughts. Today he's meeting his best friend, Austin, at Country Hills Golf Club for a day without worries. No talking about life's drudgery. No thoughts about the constant bickering and endless competition with Alisha to see who's right or what he did wrong today. Today it's only Cole and Austin and eighteen holes of the most beautiful golf course in the world. He has waited all week for this relief and nothing is going to get in the way. He scrambles out the door, throws his clubs into the SUV, and rushes out of the driveway before an argument has a chance to encroach upon today's tranquility.

As he pulls up to the clubhouse, he can smell the freshly cut grass. He looks at the perfectly manicured greens and beautiful fairways. Justin, the club pro, is standing at the door to greet him. *It doesn't get any better than this*, Cole thinks. Justin then hands him a note that reads: SOMETHING HAS COME UP. I WON'T BE ABLE TO MAKE IT. SORRY BUDDY, CATCH YOU NEXT TIME, AUSTIN. "The hits just keep on coming!" Cole yells in disgust. "I can't get a break."

Justin tries to calm him down and tells him all is not lost. He has a couple of guys who have recently come into town and wanted to play today but couldn't get a tee time. He will call and set them up if Cole agrees. Cole is not thrilled with the idea of playing with a couple of strangers. They're probably salesmen and will bore him to death with screwball jokes, tales of their conquests, and cigar smoke.

"No thanks," he says. "I'll just go home and face the music."

Justin encourages him to reconsider. "They are great guys who only play here on special occasions. I've set them up with several of our members and everyone has always enjoyed them. Believe me, you won't regret this. TRUST ME!"

That didn't bolster Cole's confidence but he relented. It sounded a lot like when a friend tries to set you up on a blind date but all he will say is, "She has a great personality!" "How long will it take to get them down here?" Cole asked.

As Justin explains that the strangers just happen to be in the clubhouse now, Cole thinks, *How convenient!* "Great, I'll let them know the good news," Justin replies.

Justin introduced Cole to the out-of-towners. "Hi, I'm Ben and I'm Don," the two greeted Cole.

Don has an incredible handshake. Ben has penetrating eyes and an "air" about him. They seem to be pleasant enough, but Cole senses there is something peculiar about these guys. It's nothing he can put his finger on. It's just something in his gut telling him to pay attention. *Oh, that's ridiculous*, he thinks as he shakes hands and moves toward the first tee.

The first few holes go well. Cole gets over the nervousness of playing with strangers and gets into his zone. He's a better than average player and feels confident about his game. After their tee shot on the fourth, Ben asks Cole about his career and family. Normal chit chat stuff. What do you do? How long have you lived here? Are you married? Do you have kids? Are you happy with the life you've created or are you just settling for what life hands you?

Whoa! What was that last question? Where did that come from? I mean, isn't that getting a little personal? Cole thought. But before he could think through his response he blurted out, "As a matter of fact, I'm not! I'm caught on this merry-go-round called life and it's just not working out the way I always thought it would. You know, the 'happily ever after' kind of life in the fairy tales." He couldn't believe he was spilling his dissatisfied guts to these perfect strangers.

"We know what you mean, my friend. We've been there and done that," Ben said. That is why we're here.

"What do you mean, that's why you're here?" asked Cole. "I thought you were here to play golf!"

"Not entirely," Don chimed in. "We've been sent to help you find the answer to that nagging question that's eating away at your happiness."

Now Cole is really worried! "OK, who are you guys? Where are the cameras? I'm on TV, right? I'm being punked and Austin put you guys up to this. Where is he? Come on out, I'm on to you buddy!" Cole rattled on.

"No, this is not a joke, my friend," exclaimed Don. Looking at those penetrating eyes, Cole knew he was serious.

"I don't understand! What's going on? Who are you guys, REALLY! What do you mean, you've been sent? Who sent you?" cried Cole in fear and bewilderment. He jumped out of the cart and yelled, "I'm not taking another step until I get some answers!"

The strangers knew they needed to offer some explanation and it had better be good. Don began to explain, "We're here to prepare you for the answers to the questions you've been asking for quite some time now. We are here to equip you with spiritual patterns and principles that will prepare you to utilize the building blocks to intentional relationships. When we achieve that, one will follow us who will show you how to achieve the relationships you've been wanting, especially with your wife. In order to get from here to there, you're going to have to open your mind and allow yourself to trust us. If you do, you and Alisha will not regret it, I promise!"

"Now you are freaking me out!" Cole yelled. "How did you know my wife's name? You guys better leave my family alone or I'll call the cops!"

Don continued, "We don't mean to frighten you. I only mentioned Alisha to let you know we are who we say we are and we are here to help you learn to enjoy the abundant life that is ready and waiting for you. Can you allow yourself to trust us a little until we can convince you of our intentions?"

"Are you out of your mind? I'm out of here! You guys can go back to the funny farm or wherever it is that you came from. I'm not having the guys in the white jackets come haul me off the golf course in front of my friends!" Cole screamed as he drove his cart at breakneck speed back toward the clubhouse.

As he stormed through the clubhouse, Justin noticed the look on his face. "Hold on buddy, talk to me," he called. "I see Ben and Don have already tried to tell you who they are and why they're here. I'm surprised, as they usually don't do that until they've played a couple of rounds with someone."

"So you're the clown who put them up to this!" Cole hysterically cried out. "I knew this was a setup! Who else is in on this? Is Alisha here? Where's Austin?"

Justin sat him down while trying to calm him. "Cole, this is no joke. I know these guys. They came to me a few years ago when I, too, was frustrated with life and about ready to throw in the towel on my wife, family, and friends. Give 'em a chance and they can change your life! I promise. I've been there and done that! TRUST ME!"

"That's the second time you've said that and it didn't make me feel any better this time," Cole said, this time with a little more calmness in his voice. He felt the joke was over, everyone got a little laugh at his expense, and he could handle that. But now he just wanted to go home.

"That's OK, I understand," Justin said calmly. "Go home and think about what Ben and Don said. I know they are legit and I trust them completely. They changed my life. The good news is, they will be right here when you're ready!"

Cole couldn't go home early. There would be too many questions he couldn't answer. He had to have time to think, to calm down, and to wrap his mind around what had just happened before going back and facing Alisha. He headed up to Mt. Le-Conte, his special place of quietness and peace, to try and figure out what just happened.

Chapter 2

Let the Games Begin

After a week of this nightmare replaying in his mind night after night, Cole decides he has to get some answers. He calls Justin and asks if they can talk. Justin agrees and they plan to meet this evening after hours at the clubhouse. Justin is delighted that his friend is willing to talk about it. He knows what Cole doesn't know and is dying for him to experience what Ben and Don introduced him to years ago.

Cole begins the dialogue. "I just have to get this cleared up, Justin. I can't sleep, I can't work, I can't think. This thing is freaking me out! Help me, please. What happened the other day?" Justin tries to calm his friend's fear and frustration. "I know," he says. "I felt the exact same way when these guys first showed up here several years ago. I thought I was losing my mind and was ready for a straightjacket and padded room too! After a few days I settled down and they just showed up again. This time I decided, since, like Thoreau, I was leading a life of quiet desperation, I'm going to hear these guys out. I don't have to commit to anything. I can walk anytime I want. I met periodically with Ben and Don and slowly began to feel I could trust them. Then things really began to happen. They told me and showed me things that I could never have figured out on my own. They helped prepare me for W.G., 'The Teacher,' they called him. Ben and Don explained to me that, 'When I was ready, he would appear.' After a few meetings with them, practicing and learning the skills they introduced me to, I was ready! And, sure enough, he showed up. Since then, my life and my relationships with my wife, family, and friends have been more fulfilling than I could ever have imagined. Would you like some of that?"

"I really want to believe that," Cole sighed. "But this is too 'Twilight Zone' for me. I just have a hard time with this 'they appear and lead me to the promised land' stuff!"

"I know," said Justin. I've been there and done that! Believe me, you won't regret giving them a chance. TRUST ME!"

"There you go again with 'TRUST ME!' I'm not sure I can take that leap of faith," exclaimed Cole.

"I know, but what have you got to lose?" asked Justin.

"You're right, it can't be much worse than this 'quiet desperation' as you called it. OK, I'll meet with Ben and Don again, but no promises. If they get too freaky, I'm out of here for good!" "Great!" said his friend with a sigh of relief.

"I'll set you up on Saturday morning at nine."

Meanwhile, back at home, Alisha was not happy with another Saturday of golf. "You work all week and play golf on the weekend. We never see you and nothing ever gets done around the house." It just seems like a broken record to Cole. *I do work all week*, Cole thinks. *That's the point. Saturday is the only day I have for a little rest and relaxation. Can't she get that through her head? Oh well, I just have to put up with it for five more days!*

Friday evening, as Cole prepares for bed, he is having mixed emotions. He knows he has to do battle with Alisha one more time at breakfast. Maybe she will sleep in tomorrow. Nothing wrong with dreaming! Either way, it's off to the golf course. That too brings on a flood of mixed emotions. He's anxious to see what these guys have to say, but he's still a little unsettled about spending the day with two mystery men who claim to have the answers to life's most nagging question. If it were not for Justin's reassurance, he would not be going anywhere near those clowns.

Pulling up to the clubhouse, he's a little nervous. There they are, smiling like the cats that ate the canaries. This does not help Cole's nervous feelings at all. But, he's here and has every intention of seeing this through.

"Hi Cole," Ben says. "We're so glad you decided to meet again." Cole is smiling but those penetrating eyes just seem to see right through him. Now he's really nervous.

"Sorry about freaking out on you guys the other day," Cole says, sheepishly. "Don't give it another thought," laughed Don. "We get that all the time." That seemed to help the nervousness a little. They head out to the course and begin what would prove to be the ride of Cole's life.

"OK, what's this about some teacher named W.G.?" Cole blurts out. "When do I meet him? What's he like? Does he ride a white horse and throw lightning bolts?" His nervousness is really obvious now.

"Hold on there. Let's not put the cart before the horse," said Ben. "Remember, we're here to prepare you first. There are a few things we have to introduce you to before you're ready for 'The Teacher.' But we promise, when you're ready, he will be here. Until you're ready, there is nothing he can teach you anyway!" explained Ben.

"How does this work?" asked Cole. "Do you call me Grasshopper? What do I do? Should I take notes? Should I have a tape recorder? Can I ask questions as we go along? Will there be a test? How many can I get wrong and still pass?" His nervousness seemed to be growing by the second.

This time Don does the talking. "No, we don't call you Grasshopper. You just listen and focus. You don't need a pen or paper and a tape recorder would not capture our voices; it would only produce white noise. Life **IS** the test but there is no bell curve. So, you don't need to worry about how many answers you miss. Focus on how many you get right and you'll be OK. Now, does that about cover it?" This did not produce the reassuring effect Cole was hoping for either. "I'm sorry. I just don't know what I'm supposed to do and how I'm to act. I'm getting a little freaked again," he explains.

"That's OK, just relax and everything will be fine," says Don. This time he seems a little more sympathetic to his anxiety. Don reaches into his bag and hands Cole a card that reads: **Spiritual Pattern and Principle #1: You have to change the way you think about the things you think about**. "What do I do, memorize this?" Cole asks. "Is this going to be on the test?" Don chuckles to himself. "Forget about any test," he says. "We are going to introduce you to a new way of looking at life. Up until now you have looked at life in one dimension. We are going to teach you the patterns and principles that will prepare you to utilize the building blocks that will come later." "Well, that's as clear as mud," huffed Cole in frustration. "Can you say that in English?" Don tries to explain. "You see, life is not academic-based with lessons to be memorized and test questions to be answered correctly. Life is skills-based with patterns and principles to be learned and practiced until they become second nature. This causes you to act and react differently to life's events, which, in turn, produces the results you desire in life. As the old saying goes, you can't keep doing the same things over and over and expect different results. If you want to be truly happy, enjoy abundant life, get to the next level, and experience whatever you want to call 'happiness,' you first have to **Change the way you think about the things you think about!**"

"So, you guys are going to give me a bag of tricks I can use to make life better. Can you make things disappear?" Cole asks sarcastically. "I'm spending my day with magicians and illusionists? Is that what this is about, sleight of hand and mumbo jumbo?"

"I know this can be confusing," says Ben. "But hang in there with us and you'll begin to grasp the patterns and principles. When you do, a light will go on and you'll begin to experience life at the next level. It is what you've always wanted but, thus far, seems to have eluded you." He continues to clarify. "Everything you do is based on your innermost thoughts, those that seem to fill your mind every day. It's not just some 'magic mumbo jumbo' as you call it. Proverbs 23:7 in the Bible says, 'As a man thinks in his heart, so is he.' The word heart literally means your innermost thoughts. As a matter of fact, you don't think in words but in pictures. You simply have to change the pictures hanging on the walls of your mind. Then you begin to act and, more importantly, react differently to the things that happen in your life. When you change the way you act and react, you change the results. It helps to put you in charge of your life instead of life being in charge of you. For example, when I say the word lemon, what goes on inside your head? Do you see the letters, l-e-m-o-n, or do you see a picture of a plump, juicy, yellow lemon? If I then tell you to bite into that lemon and taste the juice, what happens? Your mouth turns inside out, your eyes squint, and your throat tightens up, even though there is no real lemon. It's just a thought you allow into your mind, but it has very real power and consequences. In the same way, if I say to you the words wife, boss, children, mother-in-law, or co-worker, what goes on inside your head? You produce pictures that depict the image you have of each of those individuals. The pictures in your mind produce a particular reaction. If you picture tyrant, nag, monster, or some other negative image, you have no choice but to react in an appropriate, although undesirable, manner. In Genesis, the first book of the Bible, we are told that '...everything produces after its kind....' That's the power of thought, but we'll talk more about later. Does that help at all?" he asks.

"Yeah, yeah, I get the power of positive thinking thing. I think I can, I think I can," touts Cole in his most polite sarcastic manner. "I've read the book, attended the seminar, and watched the DVD. I have the notebook and T-shirt to prove it! I get it!"

A little disappointed, Ben says, "It's much more than that, but that will do for starters. Here is a little exercise I want you to practice this week." He handed Cole a rubber band with the letters W.G. ATAP printed on it. "Put this rubber band on your wrist and every time Alisha does something or says something that makes you feel angry, frustrated, or unappreciated, I want you to pop yourself with the rubber band. When you do, it should be a reminder to change the picture you have in your mind of Alisha. Instead of seeing her as a non-understanding, self-centered complainer, picture her the way you did the first time you ever saw her. She had all the flaws then she has now. You just didn't see them and wouldn't have believed them if they had been brought to your attention! How did you feel? Did your heart skip a beat? Did you hear angel voices? What was going on inside your head? Try to go back to that picture and see and feel what you saw and felt then. This will prepare you to grasp another pattern and principle we'll get to later." *Oh great, I get to play mind games all week*, Cole thought. Ben, sensing his exasperation, replied, "I know, it seems like playing mind games to you, but if you'll just trust the process and practice the patterns and principles I give you, I promise you will be pleasantly surprised. Besides, if you won fifty million dollars in the lottery and you found out I tricked you into buying that winning ticket, would you give the money back?" he asked with his own touch of sarcasm.

"How'd you know what I was thinking?" Cole asked with fear in his voice. "Don't worry about that, just practice the exercise I gave you," Ben pleaded. "See you next Saturday!" Cole turned to put the card in his bag and when he turned back, they were gone. Dazed and confused, Cole stood there staring at the rubber band. W.G. Atap. Oh yeah, that must be 'The Teacher's' name. Justin called him W.G. or something like that, didn't he? What a weird last name! I don't understand, but what can it hurt? "I'll give it a try," he promised himself as he ambled out to his SUV.

It didn't take long for Cole to be able to use his new technique! As soon as he walked in the door at home Alisha greeted him with a sarcastic, "It's about time." His first thought was to fire back, "It's great to see you too!" but Ben's plea for him to practice flashed in his head. He popped the rubber band on his wrist and replied, "I know I've been gone all day, but there is still time for me to get the grass cut before the Crowleys come over for dinner." Alisha was a little taken aback because she figured he would come in and plop down in the recliner to watch football like always. She never expected him to remember the dinner date with the Crowleys. Throughout the week he had plenty of opportunities to practice. As a matter of fact, by Tuesday he had to put the rubber band on the other wrist to ease the stinging redness from overuse! He and Alisha always seemed to be in a mental battle for supremacy. They spent most of their time trying to find a way to prove the other one wrong and themselves right, even when it didn't really matter. "It's the principle of the matter," they each argued to themselves.

Cole was more than ready for Saturday when it finally arrived. There they were, sitting on the bench in front of the clubhouse, just like last week. Ben and Don got up and met him at the curb, anxious to hear how his week went. They couldn't help but laugh a little when he showed them his wrists. Both were as red could be.

"This isn't a sadistic weapon of torture," said Don, "It's only a gentle reminder to **Change the way you think about the things you think about.**"

"Now you tell me; thanks a lot," complained Cole, wincing as he rubbed his sore wrists. Even he let out a little chuckle once he thought about it. "I'm not sure what kind of game I'll play today with the pain in my wrists," he joked.

"No worries," it can't be any worse than last week!" Don chided as he patted Cole on the back. "Anyway, we're not here to improve your golf game!" he exclaimed.

"Tell us about your week," Ben inquired. "Did you learn anything from the little exercise?"

"You mean besides putting the rubber band on the outside of my shirt sleeve?" Cole kidded. "Actually, I did begin to get the hang of it, and as the week wore on I found myself acting and reacting in a more positive manner. Although I have to admit it was probably out of self-defense from the rubber band sting more than anything else."

"It worked then," said Ben. "You are supposed to learn to act and react differently as a result of your thought process, not just in response to pain. By acting more appropriately to things that go on in life you actually avoid pain. I don't mean pain from the rubber band but from wrong thoughts, actions, and reactions and the painful results they bring. Well done, Grasshopper!" he said with thundering laughter. "Are you ready for the next pattern and principle?"

"As long as it doesn't involve physical pain," pleaded Cole. They all had a good laugh.

Ben reached for the second card which read: **<u>Spiritual Patten and Principle #2: You are not alone!</u>** Cole replied, "Doo, doo, doo, doo! OK, get out of the Twilight Zone and bring it back into this dimension for us earthlings."

With his penetrating eyes Ben gave him a look that said, "Pay attention, this is important!" He continued, "As a matter of fact, this does speak of things from another dimension. You know, next-level living has three dimensions and you can't leave any one of them out. First, there's the physical dimension. Most people understand this one and spend most of their lives there, eating, drinking, sleeping, exercising, working, playing, etc. Everyone can grasp the physical dimension. Then there is the mental dimension. Most people can also grasp this, although they don't spend enough time in this dimension, reading, thinking, continuous learning, acting, and reacting intentionally. We at least know what that dimension means. But what do you think about when I tell you that next-level living has a third dimension, the spiritual dimension? What does that mean to you?" he asked.

"I know this one," said Cole with a great deal of confidence. "I've been a Christian most of my life. I go to church most Sundays. I even teach Sunday school occasionally, when they are desperate! I put a little money in the collection plate. I don't steal from or hurt anybody. I read the Bible and pray, especially when things get really tough. I'm basically a good guy. I get the spiritual thing!" he brags.

A deafening silence filled the air! Cole was expecting a gold star and a smiley face on this one, but the looks on both Ben and Don's faces told him otherwise.

"What? What'd I say wrong?" he whined. Ben put his hand on his shoulder like a father would his son when he's going to have "The Talk" and said, "That is what most of the world thinks spiritual means, but it couldn't be further from the truth. That's why we first have you begin to **Change the way you think about the things you think about.** Then we introduce you to **You are not alone.**

"This is not about attending church, teaching Sunday school, being a good man, or just not stealing. Nor is it about putting money in the collection plate. All those are good things, but they are religious, not spiritual. **You are not alone** means that the Creator God is real, loves you, and wants to develop a personal relationship with you. Only in doing so can you answer that nagging question and experience next-level living!"

"Hold on, are you going to spring that 'New Age' stuff on me here? Is this where you tell me I am the master of my fate and the captain of my soul? I've been there and done that and don't need another dose!" Cole was getting a little put off now. "And what is this Creator God stuff? Why don't you just call it like I see it? Just plain God is good enough for me. Don't hand me this universal intelligence, transcendent mumbo jumbo. Just plain God will do, thank you!"

With gentleness in his voice, Ben responds to Cole's defensive diatribe. "I don't mean to offend your religion by any means. What I'm trying to convey is, it's much more than that. I am certainly not talking about New Age teachings because this is not new at all. New Age isn't even new! When I talk about the spiritual dimension I'm talking about how you are able to relate to the Creator God and gain access to all that is prepared for you if you simply take the time to develop that relationship. It's not about religion. It's about a relationship. I talk about the Creator God because just 'God' means so many things to so many people these days, the real meaning seems to get lost in the shuffle. Many don't even believe in the concept of the Creator God because they can't 'understand' the concept of a being that powerful yet that loving and sensitive to those who were created. How can a loving God allow bad things to happen to good people? That's often used to explain disbelief in such a Creator God. What I need you to understand is the Creator God is, God Just Is!"

"Let me give you an example. We all know about gravity. What goes up must come down. However, if we decide we no longer believe in gravity, we might establish an anti-gravity campaign and garner millions of believers. We could write to our congressional leaders and demand a law be written to repeal gravity. They, responding to the wishes of their constituents, may write such a law and send it to the president to be signed. Once the president signs the new anti-gravity law and gravity no longer exists in our belief, will you be willing to climb to the top of the nearest skyscraper and be the first to test the new law?" Looking into Cole's unresponsive eyes, Ben says, "I didn't think so! Gravity IS, it just IS. Likewise, the Creator God IS and doesn't cease to exist just because we no longer believe. Fair enough?"

"OK, I can go along with that, but what's the point?" asks Cole, a little confused about all the God talk.

"You just need to understand that these spiritual patterns and principles were created by the same one who created gravity and every other universal principle that makes the world go around. Understanding that will help you when you try to put them into practice in your daily living. That's when your life will begin to change," he explained.

Ben gives the weekly practice assignment this time. "Between now and our meeting next Saturday, I want you to practice remembering **You Are Not Alone**. Each time anyone says or does something that irritates you, hurts you, or frustrates you, snap the rubber band to remind yourself that they were created by the Creator God just like you were. Ask yourself, 'What is the Creator God trying to teach me in this situation?' He wants you to learn that He is always there and wants to help you not hurt you. He doesn't want to take anything away from you. He wants to give something to you. You just have to be open to receiving the gift! See you next Saturday." Again, they were suddenly gone. *I'm never going to get use to this vanishing act*, thinks Cole. *Just who are these guys? Where did they come from and where do they go?*

All week he tried to practice what Ben and Don had told him. It was hard, especially when he and Alisha always seemed to be in their usual "I'm right and you're wrong" competition. Each time she challenged his ideas, questioned his suggestions, or tried to correct him, especially when he knew he was right (which, in his way of thinking, was pretty much always!), he tried to remember that she was created by the Creator God who was trying to teach him something through this interaction. *There's got to be a better way! Why doesn't the Creator God just straighten her out? That would be much simpler*, he would think after every snap of the rubber band.

CHAPTER 3

GETTING COMFORTABLE
BEING UNCOMFORTABLE

By Friday evening Cole was ready to get back to the golf course. This week had seemed like an eternity. He was set to challenge the thinking of this method of teaching. He was going to let them have it with both barrels. This time Ben and Don weren't waiting at the curb. Justin told Cole they would meet him at the first tee.

"You guys must have read my mind! I've got a bone to pick with you about your methods!" he bellowed as he drove up. "This has got to be the dumbest teaching tool I've ever heard of! It drove me crazy all week! Where did you come up with this idiotic scheme?"

It was Don who tried to deal with Cole's irritation. "That's what we thought. That's why we decided to meet you out here to give you a little more time to cool off. And what a great segue into the next Pattern and Principle." He already had the next card in his hand. With a bit of a grin, he handed it to Cole and sat back to observe his reaction. The card read: **<u>Spiritual Pattern and Principle #3: Get comfortable being uncomfortable</u>**.

"That's cute, really cute!" said Cole in utter disgust. "You guys are a piece of work! I don't need this kind of grief; I can get plenty of that at home. I'm trying to get you to help me cope with this emptiness that's eating away at me and you are giving me riddles. I really feel like just getting in my car and forgetting you and the horse you rode in on."

"We know this is very frustrating for you," said Ben. "That's why this week is so important. This is a process. It's not academic; it's about learning skills over time. You have to practice, practice, and practice these patterns and principles until they become second nature, like learning to walk as a child. At first it was really hard and you fell down a lot. It was frustrating then, but now you wouldn't dare consider getting down on all fours and crawling around this golf course. It's a skill that you've mastered, but it took time. Life is a two steps forward and one step back process. Progress takes place over time. It's one thing you don't do very well because you have grown up in a Ziplock and pop-top society. You have instant meals, instant messaging, streaming information 24/7, fast food, and digital photos. You watch television programs that create a global threat, solve the world's problems, and show that everyone lives happily ever after all—in just one hour. Review the first two Patterns and Principles: **#1: Change the way you think about the things you think about** and **#2: You are not**

alone. Just because we've covered them previously doesn't mean you forget or abandon them. They are still critical to helping you answer that nagging question. You do want the answer, don't you? We never told you this would be easy! We did tell you this would make your life better than you could ever imagine. Remember that abundant life thing we talked about?"

"Yeah, I remember," Cole replied, staring down at the ground in embarrassment. "But I don't have to like it or enjoy the roller coaster ride! I just want to get on with it and quit this game playing," he pleaded.

"I feel your pain," Ben said. "But you need to understand that life is the game and abundant life is the goal. You have to learn the rules so you can make them work for you in any game. They are more important in this game than any you will ever play. It's like sports. There are skills and tactics you can employ that, when you first hear them, make no sense. But if you just apply them, you find they really work. Did you play any sport in high school?"

"I played a little football," Cole admitted.

"Good," said Ben. "When the coach was teaching you to tackle, did he ever tell you that if you hit him, it wouldn't hurt nearly as much as if you let him hit you?"

"As a matter of fact, yes he did," retorted Cole.

Ben continued, "You didn't believe that at first, especially if the guy you were tackling was bigger than you, did you? But, after you tried it you discovered that using your shoulder pads to hit him when and where you wanted to actually didn't hurt nearly as much as if you waited for him to hit you at his discretion, right?"

"Yeah, I suppose so," Cole replied. "I see what you mean."

"Great," exclaimed Ben. "So now you understand how engaging these new patterns and principles, even though they may not make sense to you at first, can be of benefit to you. There just might be a remote possibility that they can change your life for the better," he continued.

"All right, I see what you're saying," Cole gave in. "But, it's still hard!"

"OK," Don jumped into the conversation. "This week we have two Patterns and Principles that work in tandem. They support each other. Let's talk a little more about **#3: Get Comfortable Being Uncomfortable**. Let me give you a little more context to help you understand and apply it." Cole's facial expression told Don he was on the right track; context would be great right now!

"Let me ask you a question," Ben continued. "How many times do you think the average person will attempt something new, different, or difficult before they just give up?"

"I don't know—once, twice, or maybe three times if they really want it," he answered.

That seemed to be the perfect opening Don was waiting for to jump in. "You make our job too easy!" he joked. "You are the perfect setup man. I'm glad you are willing to admit that you're overwhelmed and just don't quite get it. Remember when we talked about learning to walk? It's a skill and skills take time and practice. The more you practice, the quicker you learn the skill. If you practice once a week for five minutes, it will take you forever. If you practice every day, throughout the day you'll learn the skill and grow much faster. Either way, it's up to you."

Ben tried to return to the discussion about patterns and principles. "Let's get back to how **It is about you. 'THEY' are NOT the problem**. This skill requires you to evaluate every situation, knowing that you are only responsible for your own actions and reactions. You have the power to make the situation get better or worse. You will never have to answer for Alisha's or anyone else's actions and reactions. You will always have to answer for yours. Let me try putting it into context again. Let's say you're headed down the stairs for breakfast, getting ready to go to work. You really wanted to wear that favorite shirt with this suit today, but you can't find it. You've looked everywhere. You call down to Alisha, 'Honey, have you seen my favorite shirt?' She calls back, 'Sorry, I didn't have time to pick up the dry cleaning yesterday, with picking up the kids, soccer practice, and the recital too. I'll get it today.' Now you have two options. The outcome is totally in your hands. You can go into a tirade about how hard you work, and how well you support this family, and all you ask is that she pick up the dry cleaning (which is not true!) so you'll have the clothes you need to represent the company and make a living for the family. You can make her feel like a dog all day. You can upset the kids before they go to school. You can go to work angry at the world and fret all day, which is very likely to affect how you treat your boss, coworkers, and clients and will definitely affect dinner this evening. Or you can say to yourself, 'I really wanted to wear that shirt but it's no big deal. I've got plenty of dress shirts to wear. I'll wear that one tomorrow.' You say to Alisha, 'I know yesterday was a crazy day for you. Thanks for all you do. I couldn't begin to do all you do. I love you.' Now which option do you think will produce the desired result?"

"I know, I know," pouts Cole. "But that is easier said than done!"

Don charges in with the finesse of a bull in a china shop. "Is that the excuse you've bought to explain how you treat those you love? Do you believe for one minute that justifies your yelling and screaming and upsetting your family? You can't be serious! **It's about you. 'THEY' are NOT the problem**. You are!" "You're right! I know! I really do seem to think everything revolves around me, and I need to change that!" Cole admitted. He was quite surprised to hear those words coming out of his mouth. Imagine how shocked Alisha would be!

Cole returned home with a renewed excitement to try his newfound wisdom on Alisha. He couldn't wait for the transformation he knew this new trick would make in her. This is what he'd been looking for most of his married life. Finally, he had something that would help "bring her around."

CHAPTER 4

THE FLIGHT SIMULATOR

By midweek Cole was dying to get back to Ben and Don. Things just didn't seem to be working like he'd hoped. Every time he tried one of his tricks on Alisha, she seemed to have the exact opposite reaction to what he thought would happen. For instance, yesterday he came down for breakfast and Alex, his four-year-old, spilled cereal in Cole's lap. *This was tailor made from Don's playbook*, Cole thought. Instead of getting upset and yelling, he merely said to Alisha, "That's OK. I'll just go upstairs and change into another suit." So far, so good! But, then, he just had to get in one of his "teachable moments" by saying, "I realize you had a lot of busy stuff going on yesterday and probably didn't think it was that important to go by and get my suit from the cleaners. That's all right, I realize you can't always get your priorities right! But, I love you, anyway."

"What did you say?" Alisha yelled, "Who died and made you king that I should look to you to SET MY PRIORITIES! I can't believe you had the gall to say something that stupid. I'll show you priorities. After work you can get your own dry cleaning. And, while you're at it, you probably should figure out what you're going to eat for dinner because Alex, Taylor, and I will be at my mother's!"

What just happened? thought Cole in bewilderment. *I did exactly what Don told me to do. I said, "It's no big deal; I'll change clothes even though you didn't get to the dry cleaners. I love you." This wasn't supposed to happen! I don't understand.* After a couple of nights on the couch, Saturday finally arrived. He couldn't wait to get to the golf course to let 'em have it. *I did everything they told me to,* he thought, *and this week has been a complete nightmare! I've about had it with these two.* As could be expected, Ben and Don were not at the curb to meet him this time. "Just as I thought," he murmured as he stomped toward his golf cart and sped to the first tee. "They knew this would backfire on me. They set me up and now they're sitting there, laughing at what a fool I've been, solely for their entertainment. I'll let them have a piece of my mind!"

Before he could say a word, Ben spoke. "It didn't go like you planned did it? Alisha didn't react quite like you had hoped, did she? You've had a rather long and painful week, haven't you?"

"Oh, aren't you the clever guy?" yelled Cole, so loud that the foursome on the other green turned and looked as if they were about to dial 911! "You guys set me up and you know it. I'm so happy you got your kicks at my expense. I hope you've enjoyed it because I've been miserable all week. I've about had it with you two!" Then he asked, "How did you know what happened? How'd you know about Alisha's tirades?"

Don decided to take a jab. "How did you expect Alisha to react when you basically told her that her activities and duties are insignificant while yours are supreme? I probably would have thrown you out of the house too."

"I did no such thing!" screamed Cole. "I did just what you told me. I said, 'It's no big deal. I'll go change clothes,' and then I even took time to tell her that it was OK that she didn't pick up the dry cleaning. That's what you told me to say."

"That's not what we told you and that's not what you said," exclaimed Don.

Wanting to preserve a little of Cole's dignity, Ben gently said, "What a great way to introduce the next pattern and principle," as he presented another card. This one read: **Spiritual Pattern and Principle #5: What you "SEEK" is more important than what you "SAY."** You say you want a better relationship with your wife, but your behavior indicates you really want her to come around to your way of thinking. That's not the way it works! You thought you were saying, 'It's OK that you didn't get around to picking up the dry cleaning,' but what Alisha heard was, 'You were so busy doing your piddling insignificant stuff that you didn't get to the important stuff, my stuff!' I'm quite sure your mom probably told you many times, 'It's not WHAT you say, but HOW you say it!' This week you didn't say it very well, even though you meant well. You were not thinking of Alisha and her feelings. You were really thinking about how important you are to the world you live in. No wonder she left you a blanket and a pillow on the couch."

Don decided to get into the act now by adding, "Let me try to put this into perspective for you, Cole. If you say you want to lose weight or quit smoking but you continue to stuff Twinkies in your face or buy cartons of cigarettes, you are 'SAYING' one thing but 'SEEKING' another. You will not lose weight or quit smoking as long as you continue these behaviors. It works the same way with how you think about and treat Alisha. Remember **#1: Change the way you think about the things you think about**. Instead of thinking how you can get Alisha to come around to your way of thinking and doing things, think, 'How can I make Alisha feel that I love her and appreciate her?' Think, 'What impact will what I'm about to say or do have on Alisha's feelings of self-worth?' You see, making it about her is dependent on how you act and react, not how she acts! Go back to **#4: It is about you. 'THEY' are NOT the problem**."

"I think I understand," said Cole. "I'm still trying to make it about getting what I want instead of helping Alisha get what she needs, right?"

"That's it," said Don. "As a matter of fact, you might want to change the way you think about the golden rule. If Alisha is an introvert and you're an extrovert, do you really want her to treat you the way she wants to be treated? A more complete interpretation of the golden rule would be, *'Do unto others that which is in their best interest.'* We will talk more about that later. Make it about helping them fulfill their needs and you'll find you reach your dreams a lot faster."

"That is just so hard to do," whimpered Cole, as if he were in pursuit of the impossible dream. "I thought I was doing so well, when I was actually making things worse. I don't know if I'll ever get the hang of it!"

Don laughed out loud and bellowed, "Grasshopper, you continue setting these things up just like you know the script!"

Ben added, "That is the perfect setup for the next pattern and principle." The new card read: **Spiritual Pattern and Principle #6: It's simple but it's not easy. You must spend time in the flight simulator**. "We call it the simulator for a reason," he continued.

That's great, Cole thought, *because I don't have a clue what you're talking about!*

Ben asked, "When is the first time you want your airline pilot to experience engine failure?"

Cole (again with the deer in the headlights look) replied, "I don't want my pilot to ever experience engine failure."

"I know," said Ben, "But if it were to happen, would you rather it be at 35,000 feet with you sitting in row 6-A or would you prefer that he learn what to do while he is in the flight simulator? You see, if he experiences it in the simulator and his reaction is wrong, the instructor simply says, 'You crashed and burned; let's reset it and try it again until you get it right.' That way, the pilot learns what to do when the stakes are not so high and will already have experienced the event in his mind. He'll know instinctively how to react without panic. He will automatically act according to what he has learned, and his chances of saving the aircraft and hundreds of lives are increased dramatically. This happens only because he took the time to practice, practice, practice in the flight simulator before it ever happens in real life. **You have to spend time in the flight simulator** so you will know how to act and react to circumstances you and Alisha will face in your daily lives. Let me go ahead and give you a 'heads up' on next week! This process is, like life, two steps forward and one step back. You will learn new ways to think, act, and react to move you toward living at the next level."

"But sometimes things won't go like you thought. Sometimes you'll forget the pattern and principle. Sometimes you'll just screw up! Don't let that get you so frustrated you want to quit. Remember, this too shall pass. Keep practicing the skills you have learned regarding the patterns and principles. You won't stop taking steps backward, but you will find they happen less often and you will get out of them much faster."

"So, you're saying last week was just a step backward for me? It sure seemed like a journey into hell and more than just a missed step! How do I get the backward steps to be smaller and less frequent?" Cole asked, sounding a little gun shy after last week's turn of events. Ben repeated, "**Spend time in the flight simulator** and practice, practice, practice. That is the only way. You don't get it from a book. You don't get it by attending a seminar or workshop. These are skills that can only be gained by practice, critique, practice, critique, and more practice."

Cole countered again, as if to gain the upper hand in a contest of wits. "When is Alisha going to have to do some of this stuff? Why do I have to do all the work? That's not fair!"

With the patience of Job, Ben continued to encourage him, "I know! Life's not fair. We never said it was. We weren't going to move on to the next pattern and principle this week. But now that you've brought it up, I'll share it with you and we will spend more time on it later." He pulled another card out of his pocket.

It read: **Spiritual Pattern and Principle #7: You will never be perfect, but that's no excuse not to try to get better**. Remember: **#4: It is about you. "THEY" are NOT the problem**. Stop worrying about Alisha. Remember, you will not be held accountable for her actions and reactions. You will be held accountable for yours!

"OK," Cole blurted out. "I get it. I'll focus on what I'm 'SEEKING' instead of what I'm 'SAYING' this week. I know this is about ME, my actions, and my reactions. I'll spend time in the flight simulator practicing the patterns and principles. I promise!" he said, like a schoolboy after being scolded.

"Great!" said Ben and Don simultaneously. "We've prepared a little reminder to help you this week. Read it when you get up each day. Read it sometime during each day and prior to going to bed each night." Ben handed him a small piece of paper and said, "We'll see you next week."

It read:

Patterns and Principles to prepare your heart for what is to come!

1. **Change the way you think about the things you think about.**

2. **You are not alone.**

3. **Get comfortable being uncomfortable.**

4. **What you "SEEK" is more important than what you "SAY."**

5. **It "Is" about you. "THEY" are NOT the problem!**

6. **It's simple, but not easy. You must spend time in the flight simulator.**

7. **You will never be perfect, but that's no excuse not to try to get better.**

HAVE A GREAT WEEK!

On the way home Cole kept looking at the piece of paper and repeating a little prayer, "Dear God, I don't understand this but I want to learn to do this right. Please, please, don't let me screw it up!" He folded the paper and placed it in his wallet where he could easily get to it. *This week I'm going to make it about helping Alisha know my love for her and how I appreciate all she does for me and our family*, he thought as he pulled out of the parking lot.

CHAPTER 5

YOU'LL NEVER BE PERFECT, BUT THAT'S NO EXCUSE

Cole stifled the urge to ask Ben and Don about the vanishing act that always seemed to occur at the end of their visits. This puzzled him. However, the idea of what the answer to this mystery might be frightened him more, so he just greeted them in his typical manner.

"How was your week?" inquired Ben.

"I gotta tell you," Cole moaned, "I'm just not sure all this work is worth the effort! I read these patterns and principles morning, noon, and night. I try to think about them as much as I can throughout the day and I'm just not seeing the results I was expecting. Alisha has hardly changed a bit. She is still the same old same old! We are constantly in this mental competition with each other. She challenges everything I say with her rendition of her truth and how the world should be. She lives in this imaginary Alisha world and has no idea of what reality is!"

"Why don't you tell us how you really feel?" Don piped in sarcastically. "You still seem to think that we are here to fix Alisha. Didn't we remind you last week with our parting words to remember **#4: It is about you. 'They' are NOT the problem**. Perhaps we should personalize it for you. How about this? It 'Is' about Cole. 'Alisha' is not the problem! Does that work for you? Understand, my friend, that **Changing the way you think about the things you think about** involves more than merely thinking about these patterns and principles. The power in this process is in learning that these are skills to be practiced and not just an academic exercise in memorizing what we tell you. We're trying to get you to change the way you think about Alisha to help you respond to her actions in a more productive manner. Instead of picturing her in your mind as this competitive, antagonist with red horns, a long tail and a pitch fork, try to envision her as someone created in the image of the Creator God, that angel you saw when you first started dating. That's when you'll begin to realize, as you say, 'it is really worth the effort!' and you'll notice the major steps you are taking and the progress you're making."

"That's just great," lamented Cole, waving his club as if it were a weapon. He began walking around in circles and screaming like a madman. "So, I'm the one who is messed up and Alisha is an angel. That's really the answer I was hoping for!" he chided as he rolled his eyes, like a child who had just been caught with his hand in the cookie jar.

"Now don't get all bent out of shape," said Ben in his normal manner. "Don is just trying to help you learn an important lesson so you can begin to make the progress you desire. It does you no good to get defensive. Actually, it gets in the way of you understanding these patterns and principles, which, I promise will change your life dramatically for the better. When Don says Alisha is not the person on whom you should focus in your effort to bring about change in the situation in which you currently find yourself, let's assume there is a remote possibility that there is some truth in what he is saying, even if he does say it poorly without trying to sooth the sting of hearing the truth. If you can concede that simple possibility, you will begin to notice a dramatic change in the way you accept and benefit from critical information that is offered, even when not solicited from others."

"What in the world did you just say?" asked Cole. "I have no earthly idea what you're talking about. Can you put that in plain English for those of us who don't come from another dimension? I'm just a simple earthling you know."

"OK," Ben said. "Here it is in plain English. You cannot change anybody else. You only have the power to change yourself. Stop worrying about Alisha. I keep telling you that you will not be held accountable for her actions and reactions. You will only be held accountable for yours! Quit wasting your time on trying to change Alisha and focus on self (that's you) improvement! Can you grasp the simple truth in that message?" he retorted with his own brand of sarcasm.

Don added, "As a matter of fact I have some-thing that I think will help you as you move forward." Maybe this will *soothe the sting of hearing the truth!* As he did, he pulled a little card out of his shirt pocket. This one was different from the others. It read:

Relationship Serenity Prayer

God grant me the serenity to accept the people I cannot change,

the courage to change the people I can,

and the wisdom to know

It's me!

"Ouch!" yelled Cole. "That hurt, but I get it. I see now that I really can only change the way I act and react to situations and that will, in turn, change the results I get. OK, can I have my pride back now?"

Don jumped in, "Maybe we should hang on to it for a while!" and he jabbed Cole just to let him know he was kidding.

"Can we get back to the patterns and princi-ples?" asked Ben. "We've mentioned this one before, but it fits right in with the discussion we've been having." With that he pulled out a copy of spiritual pattern and principle, #7: **You will never be per-fect, but that's no excuse not to try to get better**. "Let's look at this one for a minute before you take it home and try to develop it. As you begin to put this into practice this week, you will notice that sometimes you expect immediate results or you expect one result and get another. Most often you will expect to make giant leaps forward in your development only to find that you've barely moved at all or even have slipped back a bit. When this happens, and it will frequently, remember I told you early on that this process of getting to next-level living is, like life, two steps forward and one step back. Don't get discouraged and throw in the towel on the process. Hang in there and keep practicing the patterns and principles anyway. It is in the gradual growth over time that the power of this process lies. Keep practicing the patterns and principles and over time they will become second nature to you and will become as automatic as breathing. Remember we talked earlier about the process of learning to crawl before you walk. Early in your life crawling seemed like a giant leap forward. As you look back now you wouldn't dare revert back to crawling but have advanced to a much better way to move about world and, as a result, your world has grown much larger. That is how this process will help you grow toward the abundant life the Creator God promised. You will take tiny steps at first, but once you begin to get the hang of integrating the spiritual dimension into your physical and mental dimensions of life, you will wonder why in the world you didn't learn this earlier!

"Again, not the answer I was hoping for," moaned Cole. "It's just that I'm not a fan of things that take a long time. I much prefer the approach of magic—you know, 'presto change-o' and the desired results appear overnight! But I understand," he mumbled, hoping not to raise the ire of Don with his comments. "I'll work harder this week at realizing it's me that I'm trying to change and not Alisha!"

As if he knew exactly what Cole was trying to avoid, Don added, "Thank you for small wonders. Now maybe we can get on with it!"

Ben jumped in again, "Now, this week as you engage Alisha in your daily routine I want you to focus your attention on YOUR thoughts, actions, and reactions (regardless of how Alisha responds!). Practice all the patterns and principles as you move through the week, and if you feel like there is little or no progress being made or even if you've taken a step backward, don't get upset. Do it anyway! Enjoy taking little steps. We know you are trying and we have faith that you will soon begin to realize that the results you are getting are directly linked to **What you 'SEEK' rather than what your 'SAY.'"** And with that admonition they were gone again.

I hate it when they do that! thought Cole. He stood there for a moment staring at the cards with the **Relationship Serenity Prayer and Spiritual Pattern and Principle #7: You will never be perfect, but that's no excuse not to try to get better**. He put the cards in his pocket folder with the others and headed home with a renewed commitment to try and put the principles into practice.

When he arrived, he was immediately put to the test! (Imagine that!) Alisha was standing at the door with "the look." "It's about time," she said. "I've got a million things to do and there is no one to watch the kids. And besides, you have a few things you need to do around the house anyway."

He didn't respond in his normal, "What do you mean, I'm Tarzan you're Jane" manner but thought about what Ben and Don had said about who he needed to focus on. "I'm sorry honey," he said. "I didn't mean to stay so long at the golf course. I'll get right on the garage and have it cleaned out by the time you get back home. And don't worry about the kids, I've got it from here."

The change in the way he was behaving did not go unnoticed by Alisha. However, she chose not to comment about it right now because she was already late for her luncheon with her best friend, Julie, and Nina, one of the carpool mothers she had befriended. As she arrived at the coffee shop she was still furious about Cole making her late. "I'm sorry girls," she began. "I can't believe that man. He makes me late and I let him have it when he finally got home, but he didn't argue as he usually does. He actually apologized and promised to get right on cleaning the garage and taking care of the kids. That's just not like him!"

"He's having an affair," exclaimed Julie.

"He is not!" Alisha shot back. She looked at Julie with a scowl on her face. Julie replied, "I'm just saying." They said nothing more about it during the entire luncheon but the thought had been planted in Alisha's mind which was the intent of the statement in the first place. The girls knew that seed would eventually germinate into a full-blown plan of action to get to the bottom of this mystery. They would, of course, be totally available when that time came.

Throughout the following week Alisha noticed little differences in the way Cole acted and, more importantly, how he reacted to her. She couldn't quite put her finger on it but he was different. She liked it, but each time he responded in a humble or more understanding way, Julie's words echoed over and over, "He's having an affair."

CHAPTER 6

THE BIGGEST INVESTMENT YOU WILL MAKE IS NOT IN REAL ESTATE

Cole, in his naïveté, was excited to get to the golf course and report on his progress. "I'm really getting the hang of this," he beamed proudly. "I'm responding more lovingly and paying more attention to Alisha's feelings, and it's working."

"That's great," Ben said.

"What does Alisha think about the new you?" Don inquired.

Cole stuck out his chest and proudly announced, "She is eating it up. She's totally buying what I'm selling. She hasn't been nagging as much, and I think she is beginning to see the real me!" he went on and on.

Don added with just a note of warning, "Things are not always what they seem."

"What does that mean?" complained Cole. "Why would you say a dumb thing like that when you weren't even there to see how I had her eating out of my hand? She is totally seeing the changes I'm making and she's loving it!"

Don, with a skeptical look in his eye, replied, "I'm just saying!"

"Let's get back to the business at hand," interrupted Ben. "I know that you've worked very hard this week, Cole. I'm sure Alisha is noticing your progress and I have no doubt that she likes what she is seeing. But Don is right. Don't get too caught up in how wonderful you are. First, let's examine the progress you're making."

"It started the minute I got home last Saturday," he boasted. "She was waiting at the door, ready to let me have it. As soon as I got out of the car, she jumped all over me about making her late for her luncheon with her girlfriends, which, by the way, was totally the fault of you guys. I didn't argue. I didn't yell back. I calmly and lovingly apologized and promised to clean the garage and take care of the kids. Throughout the week when she would get on my case, I'd catch myself about to let her have it. But I would think about how it would sound to her and I'd respond more sensitively. How could she not respond positively to that?"

Don mumbled something about a black hole, but Cole chose to ignore the comment.

"That's great," offered Ben. "Let's talk a little about your assessment of the situation. Are you sure your responses—and I'm impressed with the number of times you were able reign in your normal reaction—are focused on Alisha's feelings? Is there a remote possibility your changes are designed to reduce your pain and suffering?"

"What kind of foolish question is that?" Cole shot back. "How can you say such a thing? What's wrong with me trying to avoid pain and suffering? If I'm suffering less, she's suffering less! Isn't that the idea?" he argued. Don, in his usual fashion, mumbled, "Well, pin a rose on your nose, Mr. Golden Rule Man!"

"I heard that, and what is wrong with me treating her the way I want to be treated!" Cole blurted out in frustration with the way Don was always sticking his two cents worth in. "I thought you were on my side. Why do you always have to make those smart remarks every time I tell you something I'm doing to make things better?"

"Since you asked," began Don. "Let's talk about what you're doing to make things better. Who are you making things better for, you or Alisha?"

"What's the difference?" Cole argued back. "I'm not sure I understand. If it helps her, it helps me. If it helps me, it helps her. What's the difference?"

"I love this guy," Don said, looking back at Ben with a chuckle. "He is such a great straight man. We open the door, and he just charges right in!"

"That's really helpful!" Cole said, looking at Ben for some relief from Don's critique.

Ben smiled and said, "I know but he does make you think, doesn't he? Once again let's overlook Don's direct approach and examine the possibility that there is some nugget of truth in what he is saying that can benefit you and Alisha. Remember when we talked earlier about The Golden Rule, Do unto others as you would have them do unto you," he added. "What's wrong with that statement?"

Cole stepped back and looked at Ben as if he expected a bolt of lightning to strike him down. "Are you out of your mind?" he exclaimed. "That is a direct quotation from the words of Jesus. They are written in red in the Bible. How can you insinuate that there is something wrong with them? That's blasphemy, isn't it?"

"You're right," Ben said calmly. "But let me explain. What is wrong with that statement is it is written in English. If you were to examine that statement in the language and context of Christ, you would find that a more complete understanding of what He said is, *'Do unto others that which is in THEIR best interest.'* It's not really about how or what you want but more about what is in the best interest of Alisha. If you are responding to her in a different way just to ease your pain, you are missing the point and will not enjoy the life-changing power of the spiritual pattern and principle as it was intended. It becomes an exercise in futility, and you will walk away still asking, 'Is that all there is?' Isn't that the nagging question that brought us together in the first place?"

"Well, since you put it that way, I guess you're right," Cole sheepishly responded. "And although I don't have to like the way he says it, I guess Don is right. I have been doing this more for me than for Alisha. You guys drive a hard bargain!" he replied somewhat jokingly, but they could sense the sincerity in his voice.

Ben continued, "It's great to hear you begin to practice these spiritual patterns and principles and realize you are gradually **changing the way you think about the things you think about**." He pulled out another card that read: <u>**Spiritual Pattern and Principle #8: The biggest investment you will make in your lifetime is NOT real estate**</u>.

"OK, what is that supposed to mean?" Cole bemoaned. "I know you have some hidden message in there. I wish you would just come out and say it!"

"Well," said Ben, "There is a very important truth in that statement, and we certainly don't want it to be hidden. The fact is the biggest investment you will make in your life time is NOT in real estate but in relationships. More importantly, it's your relationship with the Creator God, with your spouse, with your family, and then with others that matters most. The key to the power of this principle is in the order in which you develop those relationships. Remember #5: **What you 'SEEK' is more important than what you 'SAY' you want.** What have you been seeking?"

"I've been seeking to be more sensitive to Alisha and to help her feel loved. What on earth are you driving at? I'm tired of getting drug over the hot coals by you guys every time I try to do what you tell me to," Cole retorted in frustration.

"The heat you're feeling wasn't brought on by us!" Don interjected. Then, before Cole could come back with some trite remark, Don looked him straight in the eye and added, "I'm just saying!"

Once again, Ben came to the rescue. "Don may be getting a little ahead of us here, Cole. He is alluding to Spiritual Pattern and Principle #10, but you're not ready for that one yet. Let's focus on #8, the things you are actually investing in and the things you think you're investing in. When you and Alisha have an argument and you go to the garage to get away from an ugly situation, what's your thought process?"

"I'll bet it usually goes something like this: 'When I go back in there, I'll say this (…), then she'll say that (…). And I'll be prepared to shoot back with this (…), and that will put her in her place. I win, game over.' Now be honest with yourself, how's that working for you?"

Again, like the kid caught with his hand in the cookie jar, Cole replied, "Yes, it does usually go something like that, and it's not working all that well. But I just hate it when she has to challenge or criticize everything I say and do. When do I get to win? Why do I always have to be the loser?"

It was Don's turn again, and he'd been waiting patiently to weigh in. "Once again you are missing the point of the process. You are not **changing the way you think about the things you think about**. Winning is not about putting Alisha in her place, which by the way, you think is somewhere beneath you and your majestic highly intelligent self! Winning is making Alisha feel loved, just as she is without your extreme makeover efforts. When she does, she will begin to respond to you in a more understanding, caring, and respectful manner. That's winning!"

Cole didn't even bother with a retort this time! He knew Don was right and he needed to get that through his thick head. "All right, all right!" he gave in. "I understand, but why does this have to be so hard? Can't you make it simpler or give me a shortcut?" he pleaded.

"Sorry friend," Ben added. "Remember we told you in Spiritual Pattern and Principle #6: **It's simple but not easy. You have to spend time in the flight simulator**. That is a big part of what is wrong with relationships today. Everyone wants a shortcut. They want someone to come in and fix things (usually fix the other person) to make themselves happy. They want instant gratification and don't want to invest the time, effort, and energy required to develop the relationship that was intended for every relationship. The fact of the matter is there are no shortcuts. There is no quick fix. You have to spend time practicing the skills learned from the spiritual patterns and principles until they become second nature to you. You will make mistakes along the way. You have to pick yourself up, dust yourself off, and start all over again. But you already know that. Your mother told you that a million times, didn't she?" he added. "You merely have to keep on keeping on. It will come and when it does, you will be absolutely amazed at the difference it makes in your life!"

"I surely hope so," Cole replied out of sheer fatigue. "I hope this catches on soon. I'm just getting worn out from banging my head against a brick wall! Then I talk with you guys and realize 'I am that wall!' Maybe one day I'll begin to get out of my own way and let this stuff begin to sink in."

In his thickest fake British accent Don looked at Ben and chimed in, "By Jove, I think he's got it!" Then he turned to Cole and said with all sincerity, "You finally are realizing that you are your worst enemy. It's not Alisha or some other imaginary enemy. I honestly think you are on your way!" He handed Cole a single sheet of paper and said, "See you next week." Once again, they were gone.

Cole stood there looking at the sheet of paper that read:

Patterns and Principles to prepare your heart for what is to come!

1. **Change the way you think about the things you think about.**

2. **You are not alone.**

3. **Get comfortable being uncomfortable.**

---

4. It is about you. "THEY" are NOT the problem.

5. What you "SEEK" is more important than what you "SAY."

6. It's simple, but not easy. You must spend time in the flight simulator.

7. You will never be perfect, but that's no excuse not to try to get better.

8. The biggest investment you will make in your lifetime is NOT real estate.

EXPECT GREAT THINGS TO HAPPEN!

CHAPTER 7

LOVE IS NOT SOMETHING THAT HAPPENS TO YOU

All the way home, Cole couldn't help but feel the sting of the painful exchange with Ben and Don (mostly Don!). *This is so important, not just for my marriage, but what if everyone could learn to work at developing their relationships? What a monumental difference it would make*, he thought. *How can I keep my focus on me and quit trying to fix Alisha?* Pleading for God's help in his quest, Cole cried out, "This is just so hard! Please God, don't let me keep screwing this up!" At that moment, almost as if in response to his plea, a clear message popped into his head: "Learn to live it!" *What? Where did that come from? What does that mean?* A barrage of questions flooded through his already tired brain.

This time, with both the encouragement and the sting of Don's comments, he was a little more prepared when Alisha met him at the door. She was not a big fan of his being at work all week and then wasting most of Saturday every weekend at the golf course. *He thinks he needs time to unwind*, she thought. *When does he think I'm supposed to unwind? When do I get away from it all and relax?*

Before she could get any of her caustic thoughts out of her mouth, Cole countered with something she did not expect, and he knew not from whence it came. "Honey, I'm sorry I've been so selfish lately," he said. "I've been thinking only of myself and taking every weekend to relax and play golf. I've decided to play only once a month, and that will give me more time to spend with you and the kids and get some things done around the house."

She could scarcely believe her own ears! He could hardly believe his own spoken words! They both thought, *Where in the world did that come from?* Not wanting to look a gift horse in the mouth, she simply said, "Thank you for small wonders!" and headed out to meet the girls.

Cole stood there in his living room stunned, both at what had just come out of his mouth and her snippy response to it. He began to get a little hot under the collar as he thought about her parting comment. Just as his thermostat began to rise, he was interrupted by a voice that seemed vaguely familiar: "Learn to live it!" the voice said. *What? Who said that? What is going on?* He was a little frightened by the eeriness of the experience. *Am I losing my mind? Am I hearing voices now?* he thought.

Meanwhile, Alisha was having lunch with the girls again, and they were more than ready when she told them what Cole had just said. "I told you so!" Julie boasted. "He IS having an affair! I knew it! What are you going to do about it?" she quizzed Alisha. Nina just looked on in astonishment.

This time Alisha argued back, "He is not! Stop saying that!" But the seed had been planted. The thought was beginning to grow. *What if he IS?* she thought, though she still would not let herself say those words out loud. *How can I know? What will I do? Oh God, don't let it be true!* Thoughts now raced through her mind like a stampede of wild horses.

During the next week or so, Cole was fully absorbed in earnestly trying to be intentional about being attentive to Alisha's feelings. He also began to think about that strange phrase that seemed to come out of nowhere: "Learn to live it!" He assumed that was God's way of telling him to focus on these new spiritual patterns and principles and to actually put them into practice in his daily living. (What a novel idea!) He decided to start each day by going over the sheet Don had given him on their last visit.

#1: **Change the way you think about the things you think about.**

What could he glean from that? What hidden meaning was there for him to uncover? *This is a bunch of gobbledygook!* A mixed bag of thoughts ran through his mind. Then, just like the other mysterious phrase, it came to him! *Change the way I think about the spiritual patterns and principles. I need to start with that!*

So, he got out a loose-leaf notebook and started a journal of his thoughts. He was going to examine each of the spiritual patterns and principles and see how he could look at them differently.

Having decided that he had already changed the way he thought about #1, he began his journal with #2: **You are not alone**. He knew academically there was a God. Then he wrote down his first thoughts. He always considered himself to be a Christian. He did the things Christians do.

Then, without knowing where it came from, his hand wrote, I KNOW ABOUT GOD, BUT DO I REALLY KNOW GOD? I DON'T HAVE A RELATIONSHIP WITH HIM! HOW CAN I KNOW HIM? The more he wrote, the more uncomfortable he became. This made him think about # 3: **Learn to get comfortable being uncomfortable**. He wrote, I DON'T LIKE BEING UNCOMFORTABLE. WHY WOULD I INTENTIONALLY MAKE MYSELF UNCOMFORTABLE? THIS IS CRAZY! As he continued writing these nonsensical disconnected thoughts, a whole new line of thinking popped into his head. *What is the upside and downside to being uncomfortable? The downside is I feel uncomfortable and frequently suffer a temporary form of paralysis. I don't try new things or accomplish as much as I probably could. The upside is the feeling never lasts. I've never suffered permanent damage from being uncomfortable. Frequently when I'm uncomfortable I'm prompted to do something different, often bringing about better results.* The idea of doing something different to produce different results brought to mind #4: **What you "SEEK" is more important than what you "SAY."** He began to write, I'M SEEKING A CLOSER RELATIONSHIP WITH GOD. I'M SEEKING A MORE MEANINGFUL RELATIONSHIP WITH ALISHA. I'M SEEKING TO PUT ALISHA'S FEELINGS AHEAD OF MINE. Then, just as with the other patterns and principles he processed in his journal, thoughts seemed to come from nowhere. *No, I'm not seeking better relationships with anyone. That's only what I'm saying! I'm really seeking what's in my best interest in almost everything I say and do.*

This process continued with each of the eight patterns and principles he had been given. Every time he began with nonsensical, nonthreatening, or noncommittal thoughts, Cole was naturally led to more clarity and meaning about the topic at hand. He found this to be a tremendous help as he continued his quest to move from his "Is that all there is?" way of thinking toward the concept of "abundant living in intentional relationships."

Over the course of the next few weeks, he began to notice a difference in the way he thought about his normal interactions with Alisha, the kids, and even his coworkers. He seemed to be thinking more about how what he was about to say or do would make Alisha feel. How would he react if she said that or did that to him?

And you better believe this change did not go unnoticed by Alisha. Any time she mentioned even the littlest thing to her girlfriends, their eyes lit up like Christmas trees!

Cole was anxious to get to the golf course and talk with Ben and Don again. It had been several weeks and he had so much to tell them and, yet still, there were more questions. Saturday finally rolled around, he got up early, and headed for the golf course.

"I've missed you guys!" he called from the parking lot. He couldn't wait to report in. "I'm sorry I haven't been here for the past few weeks. After our last visit I, for some strange reason, promised Alisha that I'd spend less time on the golf course and more time with her and the kids. I know this is important and I've really missed our talks and the things you've been teaching me." He rattled on and on apologetically, thinking that they (more like Don) would ride him the riot act for skipping out on them.

It was Don who put him at ease this time! "Hold on there, Grasshopper," he said. "It's OK! We have been monitoring your progress and like the direction in which you're headed. You really do seem to be 'getting it' and I, for one, am impressed with the effort you have put into **changing the way you think about the things you think about**. We're excited to get into this week's discussion too. Speaking of which, how is Alisha taking this new you?"

"Well, to be perfectly honest with you," Cole began, "I'm not really sure! Sometimes I think she really notices a difference in the way I'm acting and reacting and appreciates it. But at other times I think she is suspicious of 'the new me.' I get the feeling she is waiting for the other shoe to drop. It's like she's waiting for the old me to show up or for me to drop a bombshell on her or something. I just can't put my finger on it. You know what I mean?"

"I know exactly what you mean," Don said, somewhat comforting him. "Remember, I once told you that things are not always what they seem.

Well, just keep that in the back of your mind so you don't come unglued when you hit a snag or have those nagging feelings of impending doom." (So much for the comforting aspect of Don's approach.)

"Don't let him frighten you," Ben chimed in. "You are making great progress. Remember, this process takes time and you've only been at this for a few months. You have experienced a few of the slipups or backward steps and you've survived each of them. It took a while but you've grasped the most important concept of all and realize that you can only change you. You've done a remarkable job of working on you and not spinning your wheels waiting for someone or something to come along and change Alisha."

"That's the weird thing," interrupted Cole. "I really think Alisha is beginning to change. She is not as critical and we don't seem to always be in the competitive mode like we used to. She is more loving and less combative. I think this is really getting to her too!"

Laughing out loud, Don turned to Ben and asked, "Do you want to tell him or can I?"

"You tell him," Ben said smiling. "I know you're dying to!" That did not invoke feelings of comfort or encouragement in Cole, but he held his tongue.

Don put his hand on Cole's shoulder and in a very caring tone of voice said, "There is more to Spiritual Pattern and Principle #1, but up until now you were not ready to hear it!"

"Oh, great!" uttered Cole, half expecting him to say that this was all a joke, a play on words, and that they had been messing with his head all along. "Now you're going to tell me this is all in my mind and you've been pulling my leg. We all get a good laugh and you guys go back to Hoboken or wherever you came from." He had a touch of fear sprinkled with a little frustration in his voice at this point.

"No, nothing like that," said Don. "But I think you are ready to process the second part now. That's a good thing! You see, the complete spiritual pattern and principle #1 is **Change the way you think about the things you think about and the things you think about will begin to change**. That's what you are beginning to experience with Alisha. She is still the same Alisha you had when you started this quest, but you think she is changing. It is your perception of her that is changing. In reality, when you change your perspective, your expectations and understanding also change. When your expectations change, the impact of her actions have an entirely different effect on you."

"OK, time for the cosmic translator!" Cole called to Ben. "Are you telling me this is all in my mind and I'm just imagining that Alisha is complaining less and just appears to be more understanding because I'm looking at my glass as half full instead of half empty? Don't tell me you're going all 'mind control' on me after all the work I've put into this thinking that you guys were for real."

Don jumped in, "Before you do Ben, let me do the 'glass half full or half empty' thing for him, please!" Cole braced himself for another barrage of 'you aren't listening to what we're saying' from his arch nemesis. Don began to explain, "The glass half full or half empty thing is totally dependent on whether you are pouring or drinking! You see, if you take the measurement on the glass while you are pouring into the glass, it is half full and continuing to fill. If you are drinking at the point of measurement, it is half empty and continuing to empty. So, the question is, in your relationship with Alisha are you putting in or taking out? Either way, it's up to you. OK, Ben, he's all yours," Don added, feeling particularly proud of himself.

"Yes, please Ben," Cole pleaded. "He is driving me crazy with his riddles!" Ben, in an effort to calm and comfort him said, "Well, again he has given you a truth that is powerful once you get beyond the delivery! You see, what he is saying is really Spiritual Pattern and Principle #9: **Love is not something that happens to you. It's something you choose**. Every morning when you get out of bed you choose how the day will go. Sometimes you do this consciously, but most often you make that choice without even realizing it. Every day is filled with both positive and negative things that happen. What happens to you (you call them circumstances, situations, and events) is not as important as how you choose to react in response to them! Let's look at a tiny illustration," he continued. "Let's suppose you get up and are anticipating your favorite breakfast of homemade pancakes and sausage. Descending the stairs you salivate in anticipation of a great start to a busy day. But when you get to the kitchen there is only a piece of toast and it has no jelly! You have choices to make. You can stand there and beat on your chest like Tarzan, complaining about how hard you work to support the family and how Alisha knows what you like and how this is unacceptable. You make her feel terrible and probably go to work with the same attitude spilling over to your coworkers, boss, and customers. Alisha's day is ruined, your coworkers' day are ruined, and your day (and, again, probably dinner tonight) is ruined. How's that approach working for you? The second choice you could make is when you see that your ideal breakfast is not on the table, you tell Alisha how much you appreciate her taking care of the family and preparing your meals and how much you really love her homemade pancakes and sausage and look forward to them whenever she has time to prepare them. You give her a kiss and head off to work, not having stirred the pot and had it blow up in your face."

"Which choice produces the desired result? How likely are you to get the special breakfast the next day in the scenario of choice #1, and how about choice #2? Every day you choose love, which focuses on your response to the other person (check out chapter 13 of I Corinthians) or you choose to put your feelings above those of everyone else and suffer the consequences. Which would you prefer?"

"Now, about our schedule," Ben continued. "We don't have to meet on Saturdays at the golf course. We could meet with you at lunchtime or after work any day you'd like. We would, of course, need to meet somewhere that is quiet so we can talk about these important issues."

Cole was excited about the prospect of more frequent meetings but was a little puzzled about the need to meet in a quiet place. He thought for a minute and then the light bulb went on in his head. "We could meet in one of our small conference rooms at work," he blurted out. "They are fairly private once you get past the receptionist."

"Good!" said Ben and quickly added, "Here is a flight simulator exercise for you to practice this week. It will help you develop your ability to respond to circumstances in a more positive manner. Each time you begin your 'self-talk,' trying to analyze what Alisha recently did or didn't do, pop your rubber band. You do still have that special rubber band we gave you when we first met don't you?" he queried.

"Yes, but I was hoping not to ever use that thing again," Cole replied with a little trepidation in his voice.

"That's great!" Ben continued, "Each time you begin your 'self-talk' and you find yourself preparing for battle or trying to think of a way to 'put her in her place,' pop your rubber band and rethink what you are about to say or do. Ask yourself, 'Is what I'm about to say or do truly in Alisha's best interest?' What picture do you have of Alisha hanging on the walls of your mind? If that picture and line of thinking is truly in Alisha's best interest, continue in that line of thought. If it is not, stop right there and change the picture you have hanging on the walls of your mind. Then your line of thinking will also change!"

"OK," Cole acquiesced, "but I really hate that rubber band thing. You really need to come up with some new exercises that don't involve corporal punishment!" He was half joking and half serious.

Ben and Don both laughed at his pleading. "See you noon next Wednesday in your office conference room."

"That will be fine," Cole responded. "I'm looking forward to it!" Once again Ben and Don were gone in a flash. Although he was used to it by now, the vanishing act still puzzled Cole.

For the next week he worked diligently at choosing how to respond to Alisha when she displayed combativeness, competitiveness, disgust, or any number of emotions he was used to her expressing when he did or didn't do something.

Occasionally he would slip and quip back with one of his usual smart remarks. Each time he would catch himself and dutifully apologize to Alisha for his insensitive remark. Alisha was really beginning to let her imagination run wild now! *What is going on? What's he up to? IS he, he couldn't, he wouldn't?* She continued to let that seed grow in her mind.

CHAPTER 8

YOUR DECISIONS DETERMINE YOUR DESTINATION

By the time Wednesday rolled around Cole felt as if he'd spent the week riding the most horrific roller coaster in the world. He had been up and down and tossed around by a whirlwind of emotions. Sometimes he and Alisha seemed to be making progress and then the wheels would come off. She would act like a total stranger who was suspicious of everything he said and did. He was hoping the guys could give him some assurance, some relief from this cycle of craziness.

He kept looking at his watch: 11:30, 11:45, 11:50, 11:59. Finally, he called his receptionist. "Trish, do I have a couple of guests there in the lobby?" he inquired. "No one out here but me," she replied. At ten past noon he got up from his desk and walked down the hall to see if they might be in the parking lot. As he passed the conference room he'd reserved, he was startled to see Ben and Don sitting patiently as if they did not have a care in the world. "When did you guys get here?" Cole asked. "I don't know why Trish didn't let me know you were here? I just talked to her and she said…"

Ben interrupted him, "That's OK, she was busy so we just walked on past. We assumed you'd be here soon. Hope you don't mind?"

"No, that's fine." Cole replied. "It's just that she is always so good about letting me know when my appointments arrive. Did she offer you something to drink? Can I get you anything?" he rattled on.

"No, we're fine," Ben said "Really!"

"Well, I'm glad you are here!" Cole cried out. "I'm half going out of my mind. Alisha and I have been up and down all week and I'm ready to explode.

One minute she is sweet as honey and it seems as if she really appreciates the changes I'm trying to make. The next minute she turns into Mrs. Hyde and growls with suspicion at everything I say and do. I'm about at my wit's end. What in the world am I supposed to do? I'd like to give her a piece of my mind. I'm doing all this stuff to help our relationship grow and she turns on me like a wounded animal. Help, please help!" With that, he stopped and looked at Ben and Don like a whipped puppy needing a hug.

"Things are not always what they seem! Does it make sense for you to walk directly into the gathering storm cloud and then stand there and curse the rain?" Don quipped.

Cole shot back, "Well, aren't you just the heart-beat of humor? I don't need your guff. I don't need to listen to you make these cute little remarks just to amuse yourself. I'm in over my head and I need help. Are you guys here to help me or am I just here for your entertainment?" They could hear the desperation in his voice.

"We are indeed here to help you," Ben jumped in. "Everything we say and do absolutely has yours and Alisha's best interest at heart. As a matter of fact, we have both been extremely pleased with the progress you've been making and are encouraged about the bright future ahead of you," he added. "You are experiencing the 'two steps forward and one step back' phenomenon we talked about when we first started on this quest for growing and meaningful relationships. This is very common and we don't want you to get so discouraged that you quit when you're close to a breakthrough," he continued. "You have to remember Alisha has not had the benefit of our discussions and is not even aware that you are on this quest. She must be experiencing some mixed feelings. She has been married to you for thirteen years and is used to you reacting in a certain manner. All of a sudden, she seems to be married to another man and, even though she likes the new guy, she isn't sure where the changes are coming from. Can you imagine what must be going through her mind?" he asked.

"I never thought of it that way," Cole said, half surprised and half ashamed. "Here I've been trying to **change the way I think about the things I**

think about and I've failed to give even the slightest thought to how this must be playing out for Alisha. She must think I'm schizophrenic. Maybe she's thinking about calling the men in the little white coats to come and take me away!" A cadre of crazy thoughts shot through his mind as he entertained what could be going on in Alisha's head at this moment.

Don stepped up to the plate again and took another swing, "I'm just saying!"

He did not elaborate but gave Cole a look that implied, "Duh, are you brain dead?" He didn't get all hot under the collar like he usually did when Don threw in his little quips. This time he knew Don was right. He had been totally blind to how Alisha must be processing all that has gone on in the past few months.

"OK, what can I do now?" he begged. "How do I get off this roller coaster and back to a normal life?"

"Just pause for a minute and take a deep breath," Ben replied, attempting to calm him down. At the same time, he knew he had to help him realize the complexity involved in the concept of intentionally developing growing and meaningful relationships.

"You will not like what I'm going to tell you, at first," Ben continued. "But if you don't shut down and hang in there with me, I think we can get you back on track and headed in the right direction again. To begin with, that 'normal life,' as you call it, is what brought you to us in the first place. Do you really want to go back there? Secondly, you will never get off the roller coaster of life as long as you're still breathing, so the secret is to learn to enjoy the ride and especially who you're riding with. As you and Alisha grow in your understanding and application of these patterns and principles, you will begin to see that the 'ups' will actually be higher and happen more frequently and the 'downs' will begin to occur less frequently and seem less 'down.' The secret to being intentional is to realize that it happens gradually over time and requires determination, courage, and patience.

You have to be willing to walk through the valley, so to speak, because what is on the other side is so wonderful you will never even remember the time spent in the valley when you get there. You've heard women say the pain of childbirth is the most excruciating pain in the world, but as soon as they lay eyes on that baby, they forget the pain they just encountered. Being intentional in developing your relationships is a lot like that. One day you'll hardly be able to remember this valley you're going through now. I promise!" he added with a tone of peacefulness and hope that made Cole somehow believe him.

"I sure hope so," he bawled with tears of desperation rolling down his face. "I just don't know how much more of this I can take. I want Alisha to know how much I love her and need her. I want her to know I want to spend the rest of my life with her in a loving and caring relationship that reinforces our love for each other."

"Well said!" Don chimed in, this time with a little more sensitivity than normal. Then he took the initiative and shared **Spiritual Pattern and Principle #10: Your decisions will determine your destination**. Uncharacteristically for Don, he began to explain it to him. "Cole, you see this one ties patterns and principles one through nine together. They are not ten independent patterns and principles but a continuous loop of life, each connected to and working with the other. Together they will give you the intentional relationship you seek. When you **#1 Change the way you think about the things you think about**, you'll begin to realize that **#2 You are not alone**. With help from the Creator God you learn to overcome fear that blocks your progress. You learn to **#3 Get comfortable being uncomfortable**. That will allow you to recognize the difference between the things you say you want out of life and the behaviors you exhibit that get in the way, i.e. **#4 It is about you. 'THEY' are not the problem**. Understanding this helps you to recognize that the gap between where you are in your life and where you desire to be is a result of your responses to life's circumstances. Therefore, **#5 What you 'SEEK' is more important than what you 'Say.'** Having grown in awareness, to this point, you are then ready to begin working on making the necessary changes in you that will move you toward that which you seek. Working on the necessary changes in you will demand **#6 It's simple but not easy. You must spend time in the flight simulator**. These are new skills for you. Remember, skills are only learned by practice, critique, practice, critique, and more practice. As soon as you follow the process, you'll begin to feel the frustration of not moving as far or as fast as you had hoped.

The misunderstanding from others about what you're doing or not doing will add to that frustration. You'll be tempted to just quit and go back to what you were comfortable with before. That's where **#7 You'll never be perfect, but that's no excuse not to try to get better** comes in. You have to hang in there and trust the process. The little things will add up over time. Now that you've begun to accept the fact that the only one you can change is you and you've done some work in that area, you will then need to remind yourself **#8 The biggest investment you will make in your lifetime is not real estate**. You'll have to examine your priorities and change how you value certain things like time, effort, energy, feelings, things, and relationships. When you decide what is really important to you, you'll come to realize that **#9 Love is not something that happens to you, it's something you choose**. That will bring you to **#10 Your decisions will determine your destination**. So, when you find yourself in a bad place, remember it was the choices you made that brought you there!"

"I understand, or at least I want to," Cole said. "I really wish it didn't have to feel this lonely or hurt this much. I just wish Alisha and I could get on the same page!" Both Ben and Don could hear the pain and fatigue in his voice.

"We know," Ben said, trying to comfort him as though he were a fallen comrade needing to be lifted and carried to safety.

That will force us to bring in **Spiritual Pattern and Principle #11: You are every bit as smart as you think you are, but you don't know as much as you think you know**. You see, you operate from your current understanding of how the world works. Just because you believe it to be so, doesn't make it so! For instance, until the 1500s the smartest minds in the scientific world would have told you the world is flat. Until the early 1900s when the Wright Brothers made their short flight, it was thought that man could not fly. Before 1954 it was thought that a human being could not run a mile in under four minutes. That year Roger Bannister came along and did it. Within ten years more than one hundred men, women, and children had broken the four-minute mile. It is believed that either humorist, Will Rogers or Mark Twain, once said, "It ain't what you don't know that gives us trouble, it's what you know for sure that just ain't so." **Change the way you think about the things you think about**.

"Now, let's get back to that 'getting on the same page' thing for a while. For thirteen years you and Alisha have been on the same page. The primary message on that page reads: *'I'm right and you're wrong. The world would be a much better place if you would just see and do things my way!'* You see, it's not just about being on the same page. It's about being on the right page. These spiritual patterns and principles will help get you both on the right page. I promise you that if you will continue developing these new skills, you will soon begin to see changes that will lift your spirits and give you hope for achieving your desired relationship."

"I hope so," replied Cole with a faint note of encouragement in his voice. "I'm really ready to get beyond this valley of the shadow I'm walking through. I do appreciate the fact that you and the Creator God are here to walk with me."

Ben began to give him instructions for the next week, almost as if there were some impending doom on the horizon. "During the next week, I want you to read the patterns and principles every morning when you get up, sometime during the middle of the day, and again just before you drift off to sleep at night. Then, when you encounter trials and tribulations, I want you to remember to read them again before you react to the circumstances you are experiencing. Don't let circumstances come between you and your dreams!" "There you go again with the 'trials and tribulations' stuff. That does not bode well for me in the next week!" Cole shouted in exasperation. "When will they stop? When can I expect some relief?"

"Just remember, **#10 Your decisions will determine your destination**," Don added. "Why don't we meet at the golf course next week? My game is getting a little rusty." And again, they were off to wherever it is they go.

Cole headed home with hope in his heart but fear on his face. He was determined to make his and Alisha's relationship what it was intended to be, no matter how hard it was or how long it took.

CHAPTER 9

THE UNEXPECTED GUEST

Cole found himself **changing the way he thought** a little more this week. He would even catch himself before saying things that Alisha would likely interpret as insensitive (to put it mildly!). He didn't always do it right, but it was enough of a change that Alisha noticed. When she told the girls about the changes in Cole's attitude, they were both excited. "He must be having an affair!" they shouted.

Julie could see the glazed look in Alisha's eyes and she was not about to leave it alone! "What are you going to do? Have you noticed any other strange behavior? Have you found any notes, funny receipts, or lipstick on his collar? Are you going to hire a private eye? Do you want us to help?" she continued.

"No! And just stop it!" yelled Alisha. The remainder of the luncheon though was burdened with the lingering thought, *What if he IS?!* She decided that she would talk about it no more with the girls, but she would keep a closer eye on Cole.

"He is not having an affair!" screamed Alisha each time it was mentioned. But it did nourish the seed in her mind. It was the kind of seed that just grows and grows until it overtakes you. She left the girls to their gossip and drug herself back home, carrying the weight of that seed Julie had replanted in her mind.

All week she, try as she could, couldn't shake the weight of that hidden message in her mind. Finally, she couldn't dismiss the possibility any longer. She didn't say anything to Cole, yet. She decided to do a little investigating first. She had to get to the bottom of this. The only thing he had done out of the ordinary lately was go to the golf course every Saturday and there was a newfound excitement he seemed to have about going there. Then, of course there were these changes in his behavior. He goes to the golf course less. He has become a little more thoughtful. He doesn't always have to be right! The girls said, "That's a sure sign of guilt!" Alisha decided to follow him next Saturday to see just where he did go!

Cole didn't have a clue! He, too, thought he noticed a little shift in Alisha's demeanor. They seemed to fight a little less this week. She seemed to be a little less critical this week. There didn't seem to be quite as much competition to be right this week. *Wow*, he thought, *I'm good! This stuff really works!*

Little did he know what lay ahead!

When Cole arrived home Friday evening, Alisha met him at the front door.

"I've sent the kids to my mother's house for the evening," she cooed. "I thought we would go out to dinner and have some time for ourselves."

Cole was absolutely beside himself. *The kids have gone to their grandmother's house! That's a good sign*, he thought with anticipation. They showered and changed and went to their favorite restaurant. It was the one they first went to when they began dating. They chitchatted at dinner, nothing heavy.

When they got home Alisha said, "I think I'll get ready for bed." Cole raced through his evening chores with lightning speed. He put out the cat, locked all the doors and windows, turned out all the lights, brushed his teeth, and hurried to the bedroom. Excitedly, he rushed in only to find Alisha lying there in her curlers, makeup and flannel pajamas, sound asleep. Little did he know her plan was simply to not have the kids to worry about tomorrow morning when he left for the golf course. (Don't you just hate it when that happens?) He sheepishly put on his PJs, crawled into bed, and went to sleep.

The next morning he wasn't so concerned about last night anymore. He was ready to get back to Ben and Don and tell them about how well the week had gone, that is, all but the part about last night! Out of the house he hurried. He never noticed the car following him because Alisha was too smart for that. The girls met her around the corner and drove Julie's car just to be safe! The girls wouldn't miss this for the world!

When he arrived at the golf course, Ben and Don were again at the curb with anticipation of the progress he had made. They were excited for him as he told them about the many opportunities he'd had this week to utilize the patterns and principles they had taught him. He also told them of the times when things didn't go all that well, but he followed up by recognizing those were probably the 'one step back' moments so he didn't let them bother him. He also expressed his dismay with the anticipation of the alone time with Alisha last night and the disappointing end to the evening.

"Don't get too far ahead of yourself," Don said. "Just because you had a week of progress doesn't mean you've won the Super Bowl! You are beginning to take baby steps and Alisha has yet to be made aware of this process. You still have some ups and downs to experience, and your resolve will, from time to time, be tested. So, let's celebrate a good week and get you ready for the trials and tribulations you'll have to face before you move on to the Next Level."

"What? Now you're scaring me!" Cole cried out, in horror. He began to flail his arms, swing his club, and walk around in circles like a madman. "There it is, again! Please stop with the trials and tribulations stuff? I'm doing what you told me to do. I'm being good! Why do I have to go through anything? Why can't we all just get along? I don't like the sound of this!"

Ben tried to console him but Cole was beside himself now. He thought the hard stuff was over. He was ready to cruise the good life for a while. He'd rather not go through any trials and certainly not tribulations. He was freaking out again!

"I'm not talking about the end of the world here," Ben said. "I'm just telling you that you've only just begun to learn these skills. There is much more work to be done."

The front nine was kind of mind numbing for Cole. They played golf. Ben and Don talked about the patterns and principles, trying to reinforce Cole's courage and commitment to the process. Cole kept wanting to get on to the next big thing, the next pattern and principle. Ben and Don, however, just kept playing and talking about what they had talked about for weeks. On several occasions he had an eerie feeling that he was being watched. He kept looking around to see if another foursome was right behind them, wanting to play through. Once or twice, he could have sworn he saw Alisha in a car parked across the street from the course. "Nah, that's not her car. I've never seen that car before," he said to himself. "My mind is just playing tricks on me!"

Ben and Don noticed his game seemed to drop off considerably. "What's wrong champ?" Don asked. "You're playing like your mind is somewhere else. Are we not challenging enough for you?"

"I'm sorry," Cole said. "I just have this crazy feeling and I can't seem to shake it." He told them how he felt he was being watched.

"I wouldn't worry too much about it," said Don, as they completed the front nine and made the turn toward the clubhouse. "We need to take care of some urgent business, so we're going to have to cut our game short this week. But we do want to leave you with **Spiritual Pattern and Principle #12: Learn to live like you were dying**.

Just as they made the turn, Cole noticed the unfamiliar car speed pass the clubhouse gate, almost hitting another car. *They're driving like crazy. Somebody is going to get hurt*, he thought. Then he turned his focus to what Don had just told him. "What's going on? You haven't invited the grim reaper in to take me away have you?" he asked nervously. Cole always tried to inject humor into the situation when he was uncomfortable.

"Don't worry! It's not like that. You just need to realize the importance of time and how you choose to use it. As Ben and Don left, Cole thought, *That was freaky. But just maybe I've finally arrived and it's time for W.G. or The Teacher to show up. Maybe now I can get off this insane cycle and begin to enjoy the life I'm sure God intended for me and Alisha.* He felt both excited to move to the next level and anxious about this mysterious guest he had been expecting since he met Ben and Don.

CHAPTER 10

LIVE LIKE YOU WERE DYING

As Cole walked into the clubhouse he was shocked to see Andre Karew, his old college roommate, standing at the door to greet him. He had not seen Andre for over ten years. *What an end to a great day*, he thought. "Hey buddy, what in the world are you doing way out here? Is this business or are you here for a visit? I hope you're planning to stay with Alisha and me for a few days. We've got a lot of catching up to do." "I've already checked into a hotel, but I was hoping to spend a little time with you and Alisha," said Andre. Cole thought he detected a note of consternation in Andre's voice. "We'll have none of that hotel stuff," he said as they headed out to Cole's car. "Alisha will be so surprised to see you, and we insist that you stay with us. We were just talking about you the other day." They continued to make small talk on the drive home.

As they pulled into the driveway, they saw Alisha standing on the steps, as if she had been expecting them. (Little did Cole know she was only expecting him!) As they got out of the car she ran to hug Andre and cried, "How long has it been, ten years? What a pleasant surprise to see you. Where's Caroline? Didn't she come with you? How are the kids? What have you two been up to?" It seemed like she was playing twenty-one questions with Andre but he wasn't expected to participate. She looked over at Cole with "the look!" He knew that "look" and it was not good. *What now? Not with Andre here! Can't we all just get along?* he thought.

Over dinner they caught up on old times, the kids, their jobs, the good old days, etc. As the hours flew by, the conversation took on a more somber tone. The look on Andre's face told them this was serious. "What's going on, buddy?" Cole blurted out. "Why do I get the impression you are trying to tell us something but you're afraid you're going to step on our toes or pop our balloon? Just lay it out there. We can take it!" He strongly suspected Andre was about to tell them he and Caroline planned to split up after fifteen years of marriage. Andre paused for what seemed like an eternity. Finally, he said, "I have cancer!" The eerie silence seemed like one of those scenes in a movie where everything slows down and the words spoken by the actors are drawn out, amplified and muffled at the same time. You can hear their voices but it takes forever to process what they are saying. "What are you talking about?" blurted Cole. Alisha merely sat there stunned, unable to process what she just heard. "My doctors tell me it has spread too far for them to do anything about it. I've seen every specialist and taken every test in the country and they all concur. They gave me about a year to live and suggested I get my affairs in order.

That was ten months ago," he added. Tears welled up in his eyes and they all began to sob and hug, unable to say a word. "I don't know what to say, buddy," sobbed Cole. "I just can't believe this. I can't imagine what you and Caroline are going through. I want to do something, to...to stop this, to make it go away! This can't be happening!"

Andre put his hand on Cole's shoulder and calmly said, "I know, but it's OK. Like I said, Caroline and I have known for about ten months, and we have done a lot of crying, praying, and soul searching. We have developed a closer relationship with God and are both at peace. We're still scared of the process but we are no longer afraid. I know God will see me through this, and Caroline and the kids will be OK too." "How can you say that?" Cole yelled. "You are in your early fifties and you still have your entire life ahead of you with Caroline and the kids. What kind of God would do this to you? It's crazy; there has to be something else you can do!" Alisha was still in a complete state of shock. She began to sob, not knowing what to say or do. "I know," Andre said calmly. "At first, we too were terrified, angry, confused, and unsure of how or why this could possibly happen to us. But after a lot of prayer, reading the Bible, and talking with our minister we came to realize that God isn't doing this to me. He never said we would not have terrible things happen in our lives just because we went to church. He didn't even say we were exempt from pain and suffering if we were faithful Christians living our lives as He asked us to. What He did promise was that He would walk with us through those hard times, even the valley of the shadow of death. Then we began to realize that dying is not the end, it's just the beginning of forever. It's really the goal line we're all trying to get to, but none of us really want to get there today!"

It was getting late when Andre said, "I probably should get to the hotel." Cole and Alisha both chimed in, "You're not staying in a lonely hotel when we have plenty of room right here for you. We won't hear of it!" Andre replied, "I appreciate your hospitality but the travel has really worn me down. I'd prefer to be at the hotel for tonight if you will forgive me." They all hugged, Andre said a little prayer for all of them, and Cole drove him to his hotel. When he got back home, Alisha was a wreck. She couldn't understand how this could happen. "He is such a good man, a really good Christian with a family that loves and needs him. Why? Why is this happening?" she cried. Cole didn't know what to say. He was as shocked and confused as Alisha. Their frustration and anger continued into the early morning hours until, exhausted, they both fell asleep on the couch. They picked Andre up early the next morning so they could spend as much time with him as they could. They talked again of old times and many memories they cherished. Andre began to talk about the things he and Caroline faced over the past ten months. He spoke of the roller coaster of feelings and emotions and the soft and tender moments they shared. He began to talk about developing a personal relationship with God and the way he and Caroline had **changed the way**

they think about the things they think about! Cole's ears perked up when he heard that expression, the exact same words Ben and Don had shared with him in Spiritual Pattern and Principle #1.

This is eerie, Cole thought. They were both mesmerized and impressed with how Andre talked about his change in thinking. He said they quarreled less because they realized, in the grand scheme of things, the things they usually argued about were not that important. He said he no longer worried about how many hours he spent at the office impressing the boss or his peers. He didn't bring work home or go into the office on Saturday mornings like he once did. He was no longer concerned if his house or car were as nice or as big as his neighbors. Saying "NO" to things that really were not that important seemed easier now. He had begun to spend more time walking and talking about things that mattered with Caroline and trying to convey to everyone he met how important the time we have on this earth really is. All day and into the evening they sat spellbound listening to Andre talk about the changes this "event" had brought into his and Caroline's lives. They were most impressed with the ease and calmness in his voice. They could also see in his face an expression of personal peace that they really wished they could tap into. The next day they had breakfast with Andre. They didn't want him to leave, but they knew he had to get home to Caroline and his family. At the airport he thanked them for listening and their friendship and again prayed for God to bless and bring peace to them. Then he looked them both in the eyes and said something that would become a "wake-up call" for Alisha and Cole. He said, "My prayer for you guys is that you will learn, as I have, to **live like you were dying**." They hugged and he boarded the plane. Standing there in a stupor, they helplessly waved goodbye to one of their dearest friends, for what they knew would be the last time.

CHAPTER 11

THE CONFRONTATION

It really wasn't until later in the day as they talked about what had transpired over the past forty-eight hours that the impact of Andre's last statement really sunk in. They talked about how difficult it must be for Caroline and the kids. They lamented about the shock, about how unfair it is, and how helpless they felt. Then, it hit Cole like a ton of bricks. *The entire time Andre was here he was concerned about us. He prayed for God to bring us peace. He wished us well, prayed again for us and all this time, he's the one who is dying.* They were both amazed at the calmness and peace that Andre exhibited the whole time he was with them. Then he paused and quoted Andre's parting words out loud, "Learn to live like you were dying!"

At that moment, he thought of Ben and Don and all they had been discussing over the past few weeks. "Alisha," he said, "we definitely have to talk! I've got some really weird things to tell you, and Andre has made me realize that if we want what he's got, we have to **change the way we think about the things we think about**!" "That reminds me,"

Alisha retorted, "with all the shock of Andre's visit I forgot, but I've got a few questions about your golf outings. Now is as good a time as any to get some answers about your weird behavior lately." He was about to get his first hint of what was going through Alisha's mind! With that introduction, Cole remembered "the look" when he and Andre pulled into the driveway last Saturday evening.

"What questions, what weird behavior?" he asked. "What on earth are you talking about?"

"Well," Alisha started almost sheepishly, "the girls and I just happened to drive by the golf course last Saturday and you were out there in the middle of the fairway waving your club, walking around in circles, and seeming to be talking to yourself like a madman! I was afraid the other golfers were going to call the cops. Julie and Nina got a real laugh but, frankly, I was embarrassed by your weird behavior right there in front of God and everybody! And all this time I thought you were playing golf with Austin or some of your buddies. What is going on?"

"Was that you in the SUV that 'just happened to' keep driving by the golf course? Were you spying on me? I was playing golf with a couple of my buddies, Ben and Don. That's what I wanted to talk to you about. What did you think I was doing? I can't believe this, and you brought your cronies with you on this private investigation!" "Ben and Don," she retorted. "We didn't see anybody out there with you marching around in circles, ranting and raving like a lunatic. You acted like you were absolutely going out of your mind. Who are Ben and Don anyway?" she quizzed. "They are the two guys I've been playing golf with for a couple of months," he answered defensively. Then he reflectively replied, more to himself than to Alisha, "It's more like they've been mentoring me on life than playing golf! They have been sharing some spiritual patterns and principles for living the life the Creator God intended. As a matter of fact, something Andre said was the very first pattern and principle they shared with me. They said, 'If you want to be truly happy, enjoy abundant life, get to the next level, whatever you want to call happiness, first you have to **change the way you think about the things you think about**. It was so weird when Andre used the exact same expression." "Spiritual patterns and principles, my eye! What are you babbling about?" exclaimed Alisha. "I don't know what you've been smoking or drinking, but there was no Ben or Don on the golf course with you Saturday. Neither did we see Yoda nor any mysterious Ninja Warriors! You were there all by yourself acting like a foolish man who desperately needed professional help. The girls are still having a good laugh over that performance. I hate to go back to the hair salon to hear what they're saying or to find out who they told about the madman I'm married to. Although, I will have to say, you have been acting differently in a positive way at home in the past month or so," she added in a pensive manner. "What is going on?"

"I don't know which to be most angry at, the fact that you distrust me enough to spy on me or the fact that you've drug those gossipy meddling biddies into the act!" Cole yelled. "And, further-more, it was apparently not me who's been smoking or drinking something funny! I've been playing with two friends of Justin's for the past couple of months and you can call him to check it out for all I care. Here, I'll get him on the phone for you." With that, he angrily began to dial Justin's number at the clubhouse. "Hello Justin, this is Cole!" he yelled into the phone.

"Hey buddy," answered Justin, "What's wrong? Why are you yelling?"

"Sorry," exclaimed Cole, "I'm just having an argument with Alisha and I need you to settle it."

"I'm not sure I want to get in the middle of a domestic dispute with you two," his friend said defensively. "There is usually no winning those kinds of arguments!"

"Well," cried Cole, "this one is winnable because she doesn't think I've been playing golf with Ben and Don lately. I don't know what she thinks I've been doing, but she was spying on me and thinks she saw me out there alone last Saturday. You are my star witness! So please tell her who I was with," he pleaded as he shoved the phone into Alisha's face.

"Hello Justin," said Alisha.

"Hi Alisha, it's been a long time. How are you?" he said. "Look, I know this is going to sound really freaky to you, but I think you and Cole and I need to talk about this face to face," Justin said sheepishly.

"Don't even think about covering for him," exclaimed Alisha. "I was there, I know what I saw, and there is no way you and he can convince me that I'm crazy! So, don't even try to bewilder me with some cockamamie story you two have cooked up!"

"I know," said Justin, "and you are right. I don't want to try and pull the wool over your eyes with some far-fetched story about my two buddies, Ben and Don, but I really think we all need to talk face to face about this, please."

"What good will that do?" she questioned. "I saw what I saw and there's nothing you can do to convince me otherwise."

"Just trust me," Justin pleaded. "I promise this will all make sense if you, Cole, and I get together here at my office tomorrow morning for coffee to talk. Will you at least grant me that small request?"

"Fine, here he is," she said in exasperation as she shoved the phone back at Cole and stormed out of the house.

"Justin, what did you say to her?" Cole was more confused than ever now.

"Look, Cole," he answered. "This will be as difficult for you as it is for Alisha to understand but, well, I haven't told you the whole truth about Ben and Don. You see, they are angels sent by God to help us **change the way we think about the things we think about** and neither Alisha nor anyone else is able to see them unless they are mentally and spiritually seeking a closer relationship with

God. I've asked Alisha to come with you down here so we can talk tomorrow morning. I'll try to explain it all to both of you then."

"Hold on now Justin, what kind of fool do you think I am? Angels and spirits? Is that the best you can do? My marriage may be on the rocks and you are talking about apparitions! I need a friend now, not a practical joker. I need you to get ahold of Ben and Don and have them there when we get there tomorrow. No hocus pocus and no stories about angels and spirits. Just be sure they are there." And with that, he hung up and began to have a sinking feeling in his stomach. *Angels and spirits*, he thought. *Maybe I am going crazy. Maybe Alisha is right. Just maybe I do need to seek some professional help.*

Alisha refused to answer her cell phone all afternoon and didn't come back to the house until late. They sat in complete silence for the rest of the evening They went to bed in silence, not knowing what to expect the next day. This would be a long night!

They awoke and got dressed without a word. "Are you going?" asked Cole almost like a wounded puppy.

"Oh, I wouldn't miss this for the world!" Alisha shot back. "I can't wait to hear this explanation! I just wish the girls could be there for this show of testosterone solidarity!"

The ride to the clubhouse was the longest fifteen minutes of his life. He didn't know what to say, but he wanted Alisha to know he loved her more than life. He just knew that she wasn't ready to hear anything right now. He hoped above all hope that Justin was going to have Ben and Don there to clear this up. Right now, he would be happy to get back to the life of quiet desperation he'd been accustomed to, rather than this feeling of emptiness, distrust, and bitterness.

When they pulled up to the clubhouse, Cole's sinking feeling fell to an all-time low when he saw Justin standing there alone. *Please let them show up*, he prayed silently. *Don't let this be the beginning of the end for me and Alisha!*

As they got out of the SUV and approached Justin, Alisha smugly asked, "Where are the guests of honor? Are they late? Did they oversleep?"

"Don't worry, they'll show up," Justin answered. That certainly made Cole feel a lot better, but he wished they were here and these feelings of animosity and emptiness could finally be over. "Let's go to my office where we can talk until they show." Once again, Cole was not encouraged by Justin's statement.

CHAPTER 12

EARS TO HEAR AND EYES TO SEE

Cole's fears vanished the second Justin opened the door to his office. He was about to yell to Ben and Don how excited he was to see them when Alisha burst his bubble of excitement. "What kind of charade is this?" she asked Justin. "You set up five chairs for us and the mystery guests. That's cute! I can't wait for them to get here. I have a few things I'd like to tell them," she went on.

While Cole stood there with the most confused expression on his face, Justin just looked at them and smiled. "In due time, my dear," he retorted. Cole was about to jump into the fray when Ben looked at him, winked, and put a finger to his lips as if to say, "Don't say anything yet." Cole was really dumbfounded now. He was certain that Justin knew Ben and Don were sitting right there. He could see them. They even acknowledged him. But Alisha was oblivious to their presence!

"I'm not going to sit here while you two go off and cook up some fantastic story to tell me. You should have, at least, gotten your act together before I got here. Now, Justin, I'm here. Let's have it. I can't wait to hear this."

"I don't know what's going on either, but I can't wait to hear this," said Cole in absolute wonderment.

"What are you babbling about!" shouted Alisha.

Justin broke in, "Alisha, let me ask you, have you begun to notice little changes in Cole's attitudes and actions at home in the past few months?"

"I certainly have!" she screamed. "That's why we're here in this silly circus of yours! I've noticed things. I've seen things and I'm afraid of what's behind these changes." Her voice was beginning to waver a little.

"What kind of changes have you noticed?" Justin asked. "Have they been suspicious behaviors? Has he been doing things that seemed to be distancing himself from you? Has he begun to avoid you, be away from home more? Just what have you been observing?"

"Well, no," she said sheepishly. "The changes haven't been quite like that. As a matter of fact, I actually like most of the changes. I'm just afraid that something sinister is behind them. Like maybe he's being nice out of guilt!" she added.

Cole sat there spellbound over the way Justin was handling the situation. He noticed the gleam in Ben's eyes and the smirk on Don's face as they watched in complete silence, as if they were not even there.

Justin continued his conversation with Alisha. "Just where did these feelings of fear and suspicions of sinister activity come from? Do you honestly believe Cole is having an affair?"

That last question startled Cole. "What! Are you kidding me? Do you honestly believe that I'm running around on you? And you think I'm dumb enough to do it at the golf club where all of our friends belong? How stupid do you think I am? Don't answer that!" he continued. Don looked at Cole, mouthing the words, "Things are not always as they seem!" He gave him that "I told you so" look.

"What? Who said that?" shouted Alisha. "I heard that! Are you mocking me Justin? I don't have time for this! If you're going to sit here and make fun of me, I've got better things to do. I expected better from you, Justin," she concluded.

"What do you mean, making fun of you, Alisha?" Justin asked. "How did I make fun of you?"

"You made that wisecrack about things not always being as they seem," she blared. Then she turned and looked at Cole as if he was responsible for the whole mess. "And I don't appreciate it one little bit!" she clamored.

"Now we're getting somewhere," Don threw in. Justin and Cole glared at him, wishing he would butt out and stop inflaming Alisha. They did not want to bear the brunt of her wrath.

"There you go again!" she screamed at Justin. "I'm out of here! You guys enjoy your little joke and

I'll talk to you, Cole, when you get home. No, let me rephrase that, I'll talk to you later," she said, implying that perhaps he should not come home for a while.

"Hold on a minute!" Cole pled with Justin, Ben, and Don. "Somebody do something! This has gone on long enough. I don't want to lose my wife. I've been trying to make changes to help our relationship. I've cut way back on playing golf. I've quit staying at the office late. I've done everything you told me to do and now you are leaving me hanging out here on a limb. Somebody do something!"

"What are you saying?" Alisha turned to Cole with a dazed look in her eyes. "Are you telling me that you have intentionally been doing these things and there is no funny business going on whatsoever?"

"Yes," Cole exclaimed, ready to collapse from the fear of Alisha leaving him.

Ben, in his calm, gentle voice spoke up. "Alisha, Cole has been dissatisfied with how your relationship has drifted along for years and he wondered if that was all there is. He began to seek the answer to that nagging question and that led him to us." At that moment, for the first time since this altercation began, Alisha looked at Ben and Don. It was as if scales had fallen from her eyes!

"When did you two get here? I didn't see you come in," she exclaimed in shock and with a little anger. "Who are you anyway?" she blurted.

"Alisha," Ben said. The way he spoke her name had a calming effect on her. He looked into her eyes and softly began to explain. "We've been here all along. You were unable to see and hear us until you realized, as Cole has, how much you love each other and what a tragedy losing each other would be. You see, there is so much more available to you than you are currently experiencing through your own efforts and understanding. Now that you too realize this, your spiritual eyes and ears are opened."

Alisha sat there with a blank look on her face. He continued, "Don and I are angels sent by the Creator God and we have, in fact, been meeting Cole at the golf course and at his office off and on for a few months. We've shared with him a number of spiritual patterns and principles designed to get him to change his thinking and behavior and to help him reassess what is truly important in his life.

We think he has done a remarkable job of putting the patterns and principles into practice. He's made some mistakes and will make more in the future, but his intentions have been pure. I hope you will be able to understand this and will join him on this quest to discover the joy and power of living an intentional life."

Justin jumped in at this point. "I'm sorry," he said to both Cole and Alisha. "If I had told you these guys were angels earlier, you would have run like scalded dogs and would never have begun this journey. Ben and Don helped me and Selena years ago to see what these patterns and principles could do to improve our relationship. She and I enjoyed a dramatically changed and more meaningful life up until the day she died. This intentional relationship is what got us through her battle with cancer. I know I could have never gotten through that if it had not been for Ben and Don's coaching before we found out she was sick. They helped us develop a personal relationship with God that was our strength throughout that dark time in our lives."

Alisha and Cole sat there for a moment in shock. Both had their eyes opened by this experience. Cole finally understood how these guys seemed to know each week how he had progressed even before he reported in. And that vanishing act! WOW! *That is still freaky!* he thought. Don chuckled.

Alisha finally gathered her senses enough to speak. "How in the world am I going to explain this to the girls?"

Don, again, chuckled knowing that therein was the root of the problem anyway. The girls planted the seed of doubt in Alisha's mind, and that was all it took to let her mind run wild.

Alisha continued, "I'm so relieved. I feared the worst and now you tell me you were doing this all for me! And angels," she laughed, "You guys sure don't look like angels!"

Again, Don spoke up, "That's OK, we get that a lot! We don't seem to fit the mold of what humans envision when you think of God's emissaries. You know, the wings, the halo, that whole cherub thing!"

They all had a good laugh at that. Cole and Alisha simultaneously asked, "So now what?"

Cole began to quiz Ben and Don. "What happens now? Are we through? Do Alisha and I continue to meet with you to learn the spiritual patterns and principles? Alisha hates golf!" he added with a smile.

"What patterns and principles?" inquired Alisha. "What are you talking about?"

"Alisha," Ben started, again with his calm gentle voice, "we were sent to help Cole answer the nagging question that weighed him down and kept him from seeing what has been right in front of him from the beginning. He has been meeting us so we could share spiritual patterns and principles for relationship building. He has learned them well and is now beginning to practice the skills that are the focus of the patterns and principles. That's where the changes you've noticed are coming from. These patterns and principles are not the end of the line. They are just the beginning. The real question is: Do you want to go where Cole is headed? He is seeking a more meaningful personal relationship with God, you, your family, and others who are important in his life. Is that something you would like to see in your life?"

Alisha, still reeling from the dramatic turn of events, exclaimed, "Yes, of course I want that kind of relationship with my husband. Who wouldn't?" Then with a flustered look on her face she added, "But how am I ever going to explain this to the girls? I mean, angels! What in the world will I say?"

Ben came to the rescue again. "Don't you worry about the girls. We'll take care of that. You need to focus on the task at hand. You and Cole need to spend some time talking about the spiritual patterns and principles and practicing the skills that will bring about the changes you desire in your life. Once you've begun to do that you will be ready for The Teacher. When you're ready, The Teacher will appear. You will then be taught the five building blocks of intentional relationships."

Cole, more than ready to get this cycle of weirdness over, pleaded, "What do you mean, 'when we're ready!' How long will that take? What do we have to do to get 'ready?' How will we know?" His frustration was obvious to everyone.

Don decided it was his turn, so he jumped into the exchange. "**Change the way you think about the things you think about**! You see, it's about you understanding that the process is not about what you do but what is in your heart! It's not about doing three repetitions of ten exercises. Or you doing things in the right order, or repeating a magic phrase. There is no secret handshake. Remember when we asked you if you were doing this for Alisha or if you were doing this just to ease your pain? Well, it's the same with this. If you and Alisha undertake this journey just so you'll have more, be happier or suffer less, you'll never get there. Those are all byproducts of the process, not reasons for it. Some of the things required in the process will not make sense to you. Some will be difficult. Some will have no immediate payoff and you'll be discouraged. You will often ask yourself if you're doing it right or not. That is when your heart will make the decision and you will either be ready or not. When you are willing to go through all these things because the Creator God said this is the way to an intentional relationship even though you can't see it yet or don't understand everything that is happening or not happening, then you will be ready. And, oh by the way," he added surreptitiously, "there is no extra charge for this bit of wisdom, but the answer to the question, 'Why me Lord?' is always 'Why not you?' God did not promise you will not have problems if you walk with Him. He promised that He would never leave you and would walk with you through even the deepest darkest valley life throws at you!" Then, as though he had just delivered the celestial Gettysburg address, he proudly plopped down in his seat.

"We'll know when! That's great. I feel so much better now," Cole complained, "just like I did when I was a teenager and asked my mom, 'How will I know when I'm in love?' She simply said, 'You'll know, you'll just know!' That didn't make much sense either."

"Exactly," retorted Don.

"When Alisha came along, didn't you know? What was different? Was there a sign hanging around her neck that said, SHE'S THE ONE? How did you know to ask her to marry you instead of waiting for someone else?" Ben rebutted. Then he added,

"God is not going to instant message, friend you on Facebook, or send you a tweet to tell you, 'You are ready now!' God made you in His image and that was spiritual not physical. You have to begin to think with your spiritual mind about how you should act and react to circumstances. Once you begin to let that be your starting point instead of the way your physical self would normally think, act and react, then you'll be ready and, I promise, The Teacher will appear. And when that happens, your life will change so dramatically you will forget all about the dark valley you're trudging through. People around you will even notice the wonderful difference in your life together."

"But what does he look like? How will he contact us? What is his name? Didn't you say it was W.G. or something like that?" He was frantic now. He sensed a vanishing act coming on and he still had so many questions. He knew Alisha was confused, not having had the pleasure of interacting with Ben and Don all these months.

"You and Alisha now have everything you need to begin this journey," Ben added. "You simply must choose to go or not go. No one can make that choice nor take that journey for you." Then he startled them when he, in a matter-of-fact manner, said, "Our work here is done! Your future is in your hands. We have to report back to headquarters now, but we'll be checking in on you from time to time," he added and handed Cole a folder. Then, just as he had experienced so many times before, they were gone.

"I hate it when they do that!" he bellowed. He looked at Alisha who was still in a state of semi-stupor. He knew she was freaking out. Cole opened the folder to find a single sheet of parchment paper and a business card. He looked down at the business card which read:

> *Ben T. Here and Don E. That,* **Emissaries of God – Creator of the Universe –**
>
> *"Ask and you will receive, seek and you will find!"*
>
> *"I will never leave you."*

On the parchment paper, in the most vibrant beautiful print was:

> ## Patterns and Principles to prepare your heart for what is to come!
>
> 1. Change the way you think about the things you think about.
>
> 2. You are not alone.
>
> 3. Get comfortable being uncomfortable.
>
> 4. It "Is" about you. "THEY" are not the problem.
>
> 5. What you "SEEK" is more important than what you "SAY."
>
> 6. It's simple, but not easy. You have to spend time in the flight simulator.
>
> 7. You will never be perfect, but that's no excuse not to try to get better.
>
> 8. The biggest investment you will make in your lifetime is NOT real estate.

9. Love is not something that happens to you. It's something you choose.

10. Your decisions will determine your destination.

11. You are every bit as smart as you think you are, but you don't know as much as you think you know.

12. Learn to live like you were dying.

The Relationship Serenity Prayer

Lord grant me the serenity to accept those people I cannot change,

the courage to change those people I can,

and the wisdom to know IT'S ME!

As they walked from Justin's office to the car, Alisha could be heard mumbling, "What will I ever tell the girls?"

Over the next few weeks Cole and Alisha talked a great deal about the incredible experience they had gone through. They talked with Justin a time or two, mostly to be comforted by the fact that they weren't experiencing a joke or bad dream. They even drove out to the East Coast to visit with Andre and Caroline to see how he was doing and how she was coping. Andre, as was his nature, spent most of his time trying to comfort Cole and Alisha. They were most relieved when he and Caroline told them they too had an experience with Ben and Don and assured them that The Teacher would appear when they were ready. It all came together for both of them when Andre said, "**What you SEEK is more important than what you SAY**." They had both been studying and discussing the spiritual patterns and principles, and it encouraged them to hear it coming from their dear friend. They didn't know it at the time but Andre solidified their decision to take this intentional journey together when, as they were preparing to head home, he put his arms around both of them and, once again, whispered, "**Learn to live like you were dying!**"

They had been home only a few days when they got the call from Caroline. Andre had lost his battle with cancer. After the funeral they talked about how they now understood what he was saying. Every day is precious. Every day you exchange twenty-four hours of your life for how you choose to spend that day. You will never get them back. In life there are no 'do-overs!' They decided not to waste their precious time on petty arguments and fretting over material things that really did nothing to bring them happiness. Together they decided that this journey to an intentional relationship was one they wanted to take.

They took a weekend to get away and do some life planning. They spent the entire time at a cabin in the mountains. They walked and talked about what they wanted from their relationship. They spoke of the experience they had with Ben and Don. They reviewed the spiritual patterns and principles and put together a plan for applying each of them in their daily lives. They discussed how each could begin to put the Creator God first in their lives. They each began a personal journal to capture their thoughts as they journeyed through the process. Each vowed not to read the other's journal unless permission was given first. They, for the first time in their married lives, prayed together as a couple. They asked the Creator God for guidance. They weren't sure what that meant or how it was to come about but they knew this was beyond their personal ability to achieve success.

When they came home, they had a rough draft of a life plan. It would become their guide to applying the spiritual patterns and principles in their lives. They set aside one evening each week to check in with each other on their individual progress. They agreed to turn off the TV, stay off their mobile devices, and not let the trivial matters of the day interfere with their quest for this intentional relationship. After a few weeks of this exercise, they both were amazed at the difference it made in their lives and how they looked at the things that happened. Even the little slip-ups they made in their interactions with each other began to diminish. They soon began to cherish their time together and protect it with a vengeance.

CHAPTER 13

YOU ARE READY!

As they were about to turn onto the expressway headed for home, they saw a ragged old man and two little kids standing at the intersection. The old man was holding a sign that said, WILL WORK FOR FOOD, and the kids looked like ragamuffins. They appeared to be maybe five or six years old. Sitting at the light behind a long line of cars gave them time to evaluate the situation.

"I'm not giving him a dime. He'll probably just go buy drugs or liquor with it anyway," Cole grumbled.

"I can't believe he would use those two little children as a ploy to beg for money. That's terrible. He should be ashamed of himself," Alisha added.

Then, as if a voice from heaven spoke, both of them heard, "**Change the way you think about the things you think about!**" Cole reached into his pocket and Alisha reached into her purse. Then a really crazy thought came into Alisha's head.

"Let's take them to a restaurant and buy them dinner," she blurted out.

Cole didn't have time to give her the rational explanation why they shouldn't because he found himself sitting first in line at the light and face to face with the old man. He rolled down his window as if to give him a dollar, but as the old man stepped forward, Cole asked, "When was the last time you guys had a good meal?"

"It's been a while," the old man said as he peered into Cole's eyes with a look that reminded him of Ben.

"Hop in and we'll buy you dinner," Alisha said. The little ones could be heard to exclaim simultaneously, "Yea!" as they pumped their arms up and down with delight.

Over dinner they learned the man's name was Scott. He had been a successful business executive, but the declining economy forced his company to close and he had been unable to find a job for over a year. Everyone kept telling him he was overqualified. The two children, Carter and Jackson, were perfectly behaved. They appeared to be his grandchildren. Their mom and dad had been killed in a traffic accident a couple of years ago, and so they went to live with him. He explained that he usually didn't take the children with him, but the elderly lady who usually keeps them when he goes on the road was busy and he had no one else to depend on. He went on to explain that he had been barely able to make ends meet through a couple of part-time minimum wage jobs and a project he would pick up here and there. Lately, he had some medical bills and that forced him to do something drastic to be sure the children had food and shelter. He did not want to give them up to the state.

By the time dinner was over, Cole and Alisha felt such a bond with the trio that Cole promised to help the old man find a job through his business connections, and Alisha gave him their phone number in case he ever needed someone to watch the children again. She'd love to have them come over and play with Alex and Taylor. As they parted ways, the old man, with tears in his eyes, thanked them both and handed them a small envelope. Cole assumed it to be a prewritten thank-you note, so he put it in his pocket. They hugged and dropped them off at a little, run down house at the address the old man had given them and went on their way.

When they got home, they talked at length about how out of character that was for them to take perfect strangers to dinner. They were both amazed and ashamed of how different the real story was from what they assumed when they first saw the beggar and the ragamuffins beside the road. They went on and on about how pleasant the evening had been and how happy they were that they were able to help them out. Suddenly Cole remembered the envelope. He pulled it out and opened it. There on a small card written in the same beautiful print they were familiar with was a phrase that blew their minds. It read: I'LL SEE YOU SOON and it was signed W.G. Atap.

What in the world could that mean? Who is W.G. Atap? How could that old man possibly know? A series of questions flooded both their minds. His words of I'll see you soon they assumed meant that that The Teacher, whoever that was, had now declared them worthy of an audience. "W.G., what is that?" Alisha asked. "Is that a secret code? Are those the old man's initials? Is he The Teacher? Are we ready? When will he appear next? How will we know?" A torrent of questions flooded her mind.

"I think Ben said those were The Teacher's initials," Cole said.

Simultaneously they yelled aloud, "The old man!" and they raced out to the car. *Finally, we'll get the answers to our questions about where we go from here* they were both thinking. *We had him right in our car and had no idea!* All the way to the old house their hearts pounded as they anticipated meeting The Teacher face to face.

As they walked up to the old house, they could see no lights and could hear no sounds coming from inside. *That's strange*, they thought, *for a home with two small children living there*. They knocked on the door. No one answered. They went around back and knocked. Again, there was no answer. They peeked in the windows and could see no movement inside. "It has only been an hour or so since we dropped them off, but I guess they've gone out to beg some more," they concluded. Just as they were about to leave, the next-door neighbor called out, "Can I help you?"

"Oh no," said Cole. "We were just looking for the old gentleman and the two kids who live here. We're friends," he added, mostly to remove suspicion from their peeking into the windows and walking around back.

"I'm sorry," the neighbor said, "but that house has been vacant for years. The young couple who lived there, along with their two children, Carter and Jackson, were killed in an accident while they were on vacation. It was terrible. We loved having them as neighbors and the children, they were just darling. They had no known relatives, so the house has remained vacant and has gotten run down because the estate is still in probate."

In a state of utter shock, they thanked him and headed back home.

"What is going on here?" babbled Cole. "I don't understand what's happening! I know we just had dinner with that old man and those kids. They ate like there was no tomorrow and I paid the tab. I'm not losing my mind!"

"Maybe they, too, were angels sent by God to guide us," interjected Alisha in an attempt to calm Cole.

"Do angels eat a plate of lasagna and two bowls of cheese and macaroni and drink raspberry tea and chocolate milkshakes?" he argued.

That was "the night that never was" at the Gastone house. They asked questions, threw out possible explanations, and got no closer to answers that made sense. Finally, they drifted off to sleep on the couch, again! The next day they each headed off to their respective responsibilities with the same confusion running through their minds as the night before. But there was one difference this morning. Neither of them had any doubt they would soon discover what lay behind the mystery. They fully believed, as the card so succinctly put it, "You are ready!" They both fully expected The Teacher to appear soon! And they were committed to go on this journey together, wherever it took them.

Little did they know life's roller coaster ride was not over. They seemed a little on edge over the next few weeks. Every day they would wake up thinking, *Is this the day?* But, day after day for weeks, The Teacher didn't show. They were beginning to get a little discouraged and soon began to get on each other's nerves as they anticipated "The Event."

Every time they saw an old man standing by the road selling papers, they would stop to make a purchase. They expected it to be him, but time after time they were disappointed. Once there was a man with two children standing on the street corner. They excitedly sped to the intersection, only to find an older gentleman with his grandchildren just waiting for the light to change.

They began to get on each other's nerves, each trying to explain how something the other was doing was keeping The Teacher from appearing.

"If you weren't so picky about everything," Cole would accuse.

"Well, if you didn't think you had all the answers," Alisha would say in her defense. Without realizing it, they began the downward spiral of what Ben and Don called the one step backward process.

One day, while they were engaged in an intense discussion of who was causing the delay, there came a knock on the door. It was Bobby, the mailman. You know, the one who is always leaving their mail in the neighbor's box and the neighbor's mail in their box? Embarrassed, he said, "I'm sorry, but this letter was intended for you. I found it under the seat of my mail truck. I don't know how long it has been there, but I wanted to get it to you right away!" With that, he turned and walked briskly back to his truck as if he didn't want to get scolded again for mixing up their mail.

The letter was from Andre. It had been postmarked two days before he died. "That was months ago!" exclaimed Alisha as she tore open the envelope. Inside was a brief note written with what appeared to be a shaky hand. It read:

Cole and Alisha,

I know you are going through some difficult times right now. It seems like The Teacher will never show up. You will begin to doubt if you are ready and maybe even blame each other for his delay. Let me encourage you to remain together on this quest.

*Remember, **Change the way you think about the things you think about!***

"When you are ready The Teacher will appear" doesn't mean when you are ready individually. It means being ready together, "The two shall become one!" His appearance will be in different ways at different times. It will often be in ways and at times you aren't expecting.

*Don't be discouraged, remain in your love for each other as you seek and remember, **"What you 'SEEK' is more important than what you 'SAY'!"***

Please check in with Caroline from time to time for me and don't ever forget, I love you both and am grateful for your friendship.

I'll see you on the other side, Andre.

As if their thoughts had been orchestrated, they looked at each other and proclaimed, "Caroline! We have been so foolish and selfish. We haven't checked in with Caroline since the funeral. We have been so wrapped up in ourselves that we've totally forgotten about what she must be feeling." That very weekend they planned to have the kids stay with Alisha's parents while they drove up to visit her.

They discovered that Caroline had sold the big house and moved a few miles away to a small town called Pleasant Hill. Although it was as quaint as its name, the little town was so far off the beaten path it seemed as if they had stepped back in time. Dirt roads with ruts and holes that seemed like craters lined the way. Picturesque pastures with cows, barns, small houses surrounded by picket fences, and mailboxes atop crooked little posts were everywhere they looked. Any minute they expected to see a mailbox with the name Norman Rockwell painted on it.

Caroline was grateful for their visit. She talked about how difficult it was at first, but then how the memories of their wonderful times together seemed to overshadow the hurt in her heart. She said she was more blessed by the time they had than depressed by having to live without him. As a matter of fact, she said it seemed as if he was still right there with her every day. It seemed to get a little better each day and she was OK. They hugged, prayed with her, and headed home.

As they drove, for what seemed like forever, down the winding dirt road that led from Caroline's to the interstate, they suddenly felt the car lurch and the engine stopped. Cole tried to start it, but nothing happened. It made a weird noise but would not start.

"That's just great!" Alisha exclaimed. "We're out here in the middle of nowhere and I'll bet there's not a mechanic or tow truck within miles of this place."

Cole told her not to panic and pulled out his cell phone to call for help.

"Wouldn't you know it!" he exclaimed. "No signal! We're so far back in the woods they have to pipe sunshine in here!" he bellowed with disgust. "We'll have to walk back to Caroline's and have her call for help."

They had been walking for about ten minutes when Alisha spotted what appeared to be a farm truck in the distance. She could see the cloud of dust approaching and was excited that help was on the way. "Let's just stop here and wait for that truck," she said.

"Makes sense to me," he answered and they sat down on a nearby log. As the truck came nearer their hope grew. Then the truck blew right by them, leaving them coughing and spitting dust and dirt as they looked on in bewilderment. "I hope your wheels fall off and you run into the ditch!" yelled Cole as he shook his fist at the insensitive farmer who was oblivious to their plight. They discussed for a few minutes how rude, crude, and ill refined the old farmer was. They were just warming up with the comments about the cultural deficiencies that existed in these backwoods people when Alisha thought she heard that old jalopy approaching again.

Sure enough, the old farmer drove up, and this time he stopped. "That your car down the road a piece?" the old farmer asked. "I'm sorry, I thought you folks were just out for a walk and enjoying the scenery when I saw you sitting there on that log. Can I give you a lift?" he continued apologetically.

Feeling a little ashamed of the comments he'd made, Cole happily responded, "We would appreciate it! Is there a garage or tow truck anywhere near here?" he asked.

"Well, ole Lamonte does most of the rescue work 'round here. His place is a few miles down River Road up in the holler. Hop in and I'll run you over there. This ole rattle trap ain't much to look at, but she'll get you there," he continued.

Cole opened the door to the old truck and Alisha started to climb in when, there on the seat of the truck, she was suddenly face to face with a snow-white border collie about the size of a small horse.

"Oh, don't pay no 'tention to Glazier. He don't bite," he laughed. That didn't make Alisha feel any better, but they piled onto the front seat with the old man and the dog anyway. Alisha detected the faint odor of farm animals. At least that's what she attributed the odor to. She wasn't one to look a gift horse in the mouth, so she held her breath as best she could and said nothing.

They exchanged pleasantries as they drove along the bumpy, dusty road. The old man finally asked the ultimate question. "You folks ain't from 'round here, are you?" he said. "What brings you to these parts?" he added, not in a prying way but only in the course of conversation.

"No, we're from Nashville, Tennessee," Cole chuckled. "Our friend recently moved here and we were visiting for the weekend. We're headed home and our car broke down and, well, here we are!" "Oh, you mean the widow Caroline up on Lizard Lick Road? Nice lady. Terrible thing, her husband passing and all," he added.

"How did you know we were visiting her?" Alisha quizzed. "She couldn't have been here more than a few weeks, maybe a month!"

"This is a small community; not much goes on without everyone knowing," he laughed. Then he added, "We kinda look after each other up here. I've been by a time or two just to check on her and see if she needed anything."

"That's nice," Alisha said with a little uneasiness in her voice. Suddenly, the old man said, "We're here." They turned into a narrow gate, drove through a small stand of cedar trees, and pulled up in front of an old farmhouse with a huge barn out back. Hand painted in white above the door of the old barn was LAMONTE'S TOW AND JUNKYARD. Scattered around the barnyard were a number of old vehicles that certainly fit the description. Parked inside was what appeared to be a tow truck from a time long ago and a place far away. Cole and Alisha looked at each other with fear and uncertainty. They saw a rotund gentleman with a Santa Claus looking beard coming out of the barn, so they stepped out of the truck. "That's Lamonte," the old farmer said.

They thanked the old gentleman for the ride and offered to pay him. "Wouldn't think of taking anything for helping folks in need," he said, almost as if he was offended by the offer. As he spoke, Cole looked into his eyes and thought, *He looks familiar.* Then as he drove away, he stuck his head out the window and yelled back at Cole, "Don't worry, things aren't always what they seem!" as he disappeared in a cloud of dust, just as he had entered their lives.

"What did he just say?" asked Cole. "That sounded like something Don said to me. That's weird."

Just then, Lamonte stuck out a greasy hand and said, "I'm Lamonte. I see you've met our resident Good Samaritan."

"I'm Cole Gastone and this is my wife Alisha. Pleased to meet you. Our car broke down and that old farmer said you were the one who could help us." he responded. "What do you mean by resident Good Samaritan? Who is that guy anyway?"

"Oh, that's just W.G." Lamonte responded. "He's always helping folks find their way when they're lost," he added.

"W.G. who? What's his last name?" Cole inquired. "Well, I don't rightly know his last name. Don't recall ever hearing him say," Lamonte said. "He just seems to show up and help folks out when they need it most. We kinda get used to him being there when we need him," he added.

"Well, where does he live?" asked Cole. "We really need to talk to him before we head home."

Alisha jumped in at this point, "Let's not put the cart before the horse, honey! We need to get our car repaired first before we go off on some wild goose chase."

Having gotten their collective wits about them, they went with Lamonte to retrieve their car. He looked at it and discovered it was just a loose wire on the starter and was able to fix it quickly. Lamonte also refused to take payment for helping them. He just said, "One day you'll have a chance to return the favor for someone else. Just pass it on!"

Cole and Alisha thanked him for his rescue and his generosity. Then Cole resumed his query. "Now, where did you say this W.G. what's his name lives?"

"Well," replied Lamonte, "I ain't never been to his place but I hear he lives up on Grandfather Mountain. It's not easy to get up there. Ain't many roads and not many folks live on that mountain. Most of the time there is a cloudy mist on that mountain making it hard to get around, so most folks just steer clear."

Just as Cole was about to head up the mountain, he pulled down the visor to shield his eyes from the sun. As he did, a small card fell onto the seat between him and Alisha.

Alisha picked it up and read it aloud. THANKS FOR PUTTING CAROLINE AHEAD OF YOUR OWN DESIRES. NOW YOU ARE READY. I WILL SEE YOU VERY SOON!" It too was signed, W.G. Atap.

"This is just weirding me out! What are we supposed to do now?" Cole said. "Me too!" exclaimed Alisha. "I guess we just go home and keep putting the needs of others ahead of our desires like he said. He will see us 'VERY' soon."

Chapter 14

Now We Begin

The next day they both were walking on pins and needles. They looked into the eyes of every stranger they met, thinking, *Is this him? Does he have something to tell me or give me?* The anticipation was killing them. Alisha arrived home after Cole. She went to the mailbox and came back with a manila envelope with both their names on it. It was the same beautiful print that was on the card given to them by the old man selling newspapers on the street corner. They could hardly wait to tear it open!

Inside was another card which read: Thanks for feeding us and thanks for caring for Caroline enough to go and check on her. I am looking forward to our journey together.

"Is that all there is?" moaned Cole. Before he could complain further, the doorbell rang. He suspended his frustration to answer the door. As he approached it, Alisha peeked out the window. She was astonished to see the old farmer's beat-up jalopy of a truck sitting in front of their house. When Cole opened the door, he was flabbergasted to see both the old farmer and the street corner paper salesman standing there. He was one in the same.

"I should have known!" yelled Cole. "I thought I had seen you somewhere before!" He calmed down enough to invite the old man into their home.

As the old man stepped into the living room where Alisha was standing with her mouth wide open, he turned to Cole and said, "I see we've come full circle!"

"What do you mean?" inquired Cole.

"Well, that question you raised about the card in the envelope is the same question that started you on this journey in the first place. I would have thought that by now you would know that is definitely not all there is!" he added with a little chuckle.

"I see what you mean," Cole responded, somewhat embarrassed, realizing what little progress he had made with all that had transpired over the past six months.

"That's OK," he said. "I find that most humans have a difficult time making the transition from the intellectual and physical world, where they live most of their lives, to the spiritual dimension where I hoped they would learn to live both in the here and now and in the hereafter when that time comes. Yet so few ever get the hang of it before they enter into the next life," he added.

Both Cole and Alisha noticed that, although his voice was the same, the old man spoke with neither the broken English nor the country twang he had when they encountered him both on the street and in the hills of North Carolina. That didn't matter though. They knew who he was and were so anxious to hear what he had to share with them.

He began, "I'm delighted you have been working on the patterns and principles Ben and Don shared with you. Keep them handy for quick reference. You will need to continue spending time in the flight simulator practicing those skills as we proceed to the next phase of your quest. I will meet with you each week to begin sharing with you the **Five Building Blocks to Intentional Relationships**. You will need to employ the skills learned from the spiritual patterns and principles in applying the five building blocks to develop the relationships you desire. I will need you to agree to three key terms if we are to enter into this journey together.

First: I will need you both to commit to being physically and mentally present with me when we visit.

Second: I will need you to have the children cared for during each of our visits. That way, you can give your undivided attention to learning these five critical building blocks.

Third: Each week I will give you a set of flight simulator exercises.

I need you both to commit to spending time practicing them. Can we agree on these terms?" Although they both had a tinge of discomfort, they readily agreed. After all, this is what they had been "SEEKING," and they were not about to let anything get in the way of that search.

"Then, that's it," he declared. "We begin the same time, same place Saturday. See you then!" And just as with Ben and Don, he was gone. Cole and Alisha stood there in their living room staring out the window, wondering what just happened and what the neighbors would think of their guest in the beat-up old truck. However, that did not detract from the excitement they both felt as they prepared for bed and rehashed the events of the day. They could hardly contain themselves during the next week. Saturday seemed as though it was a lifetime away. You know, like Christmas seemed each year when you were a child!

CHAPTER 15

UNDERSTANDING, RESPECT, AND TRUST

They both awakened before sunrise Saturday morning. They hardly slept the night before. The anticipation of The Teacher's arrival was killing them. Finally, the doorbell rang. It was Alisha who ran to the door this time. Imagine her surprise when she was greeted by a young man in uniform. "Hi, I have a special delivery for Cole and Alisha Gastone," he said politely.

"I'm she," is all Alisha could muster, trying to hide her disappointment. She signed for the envelope and closed the door. Inside was a card. Written in the usual beautiful print were the words: **Building Block #1: Understanding, Respect, and Trust.** They looked at each other as if they had been struck by lightning.

"What?" cried Cole. "Are we still playing games? I thought we were past this! Is there anything else in there? Are there more instructions? What are we supposed to do with this?" His frustration was mounting. Alisha stood there in shock. After what seemed like an eternity, they began to talk about the card and what it could possibly mean.

"This seems so elementary," began Cole. "I don't understand what we're supposed to do. Are we to Google these, write a paper, make a presentation? Will we be quizzed on the meaning or how well we know these things?"

Alisha responded with a great deal of uncertainty, "Maybe he wants us to talk about these three things and how they apply to our lives. I think he's testing us."

They decided to go to their favorite coffee shop and talk about the card and the three words. As they sat at the booth drinking their double Latte and Mocha Frappuccino, they were constantly interrupted by the noise and vibrations coming from the booth behind them. Apparently, there were children in the booth and they were constantly kicking the seats and bouncing around, breaking Cole's and Alisha's trains of thought.

As they pushed through the interruptions, they tried to focus on **Understanding, Respect, and Trust.** "I think we are ahead of the game if these are three of the five building blocks," Cole proudly proclaimed. "We understand each other perfectly. I know what you're going to say before you say it most of the time. You know what is on my mind sometimes before I do. And we certainly respect each other. We do things for each other all the time, and I don't think either of us believes for one minute (anymore) that we would cheat on each other!" he continued. "For Pete's sake, we've been together for over thirteen years."

Just as Alisha was about to respond, a beautiful young woman walked through the door and headed toward them. They both sat mesmerized by her radiance. That was not normally a word they would use to describe someone, but that was the only word that seemed to fit! It was more than simply physical beauty. There was something about her they couldn't easily describe. She was looking directly into their eyes and had the most angelic smile and gleam in her eyes. They sat spellbound as she approached.

She walked slowly past their table and stopped at the booth behind them. "Hi, boys," they overheard her say. "I've missed you. Be good and say thank you."

"We have to be going," she said, and the two children who had been making all the noise politely said, "Thank you" to the old gentleman (they assumed was the grandfather) and walked out with the young woman. The boys looked vaguely familiar. They seemed to be approximately five- and six-years-old and reminded them of the ragamuffins they had taken to lunch with the old man on the street corner.

Cole jumped up from his seat and immediately turned to the booth behind him. There smiling like a Cheshire cat, sat W.G. "What is going on?" Cole grilled him. "Who was that young woman? Are those your grandsons? How long have you been here?" He was visibly rattled.

Alisha was wondering what was going on. "Are you following us?" she asked. "Is this some kind of game? Are we being tested?" she continued in frustration.

The old man calmly replied, "She is their mother. They are not my grandsons, but they are all my children. I was here long before you got here. I'm not following you, but I always know where you are and what you're up to. This is a game called life and life is the test. Does that about cover everything?" He then looked at them as if to say, "Now that I have your attention...."

"What in the world is going on?" cried Cole. "I just don't get it! Why the charade? Why all the games?"

W.G. stopped him to explain, "I need you to understand something. I really want you to learn to **Change the way you think about the things you think about.** When you think about **Understanding, Respect, and Trust**, you think as if you are only human. You often use that to excuse many of your shortcomings!" he said, almost as if he were chastising them as a father would a child. "The fact of the matter is, you are not only human. You were created first and foremost in the image of the Creator God and then given a physical body in order to experience life here on earth for a brief time. This was not intended to limit your life experience but to help you experience life abundantly."

As they sat back down at the booth, he continued. "You think you understand each other because you can tell what each other is thinking much of the time. You believe you respect and trust each other because you have managed to stay together for thirteen years. Those are, indeed, statements of fact, but it is such a limited view of what was intended for you. Understanding is not about knowing what each other is thinking. It's not about understanding 'why' your spouse is the way he or she is but understanding 'that' they are that way. It's about how what you are thinking and doing impacts the other. Respect is not about a feeling you have toward each other but about how you make each other feel. You struggle to regain that feeling of 'being in love' when you should focus on how to make your mate know love and feel loved. Trust is not about feeling like your spouse will not cheat on you. It's about getting to know each other so well that you can openly and intentionally share with each other your dreams, fears, frustrations, failures, and shortcomings without fear of starting World War III or wondering if your spouse will use that against you. Can you truly share what you are feeling and thinking with each other without worrying if he or she will make fun of you?"

"Will they use that shortcoming as a weapon to hurt you when you are most vulnerable? Will your mistakes show up on social media tonight? When you're out with your friends, do you speak of each other with respect or do you make sarcastic jokes about your spouse? Little jabs that you think are harmless, even funny, but your spouse is secretly hurt by those comments. You see, I want you to think about **Understanding, Respect, and Trust** as one of the five building blocks, not three. They are so integrated and so codependent they must function as one in the effort to live intentionally."

Cole and Alisha were numb from the incredible experience. They realized the woman and the two little boys were Carter and Jackson and their mom who had been killed in that car accident several years ago. They realized that W.G. was obviously not from this world just because of the way he talked, not to mention his appearing and vanishing act! They were trying to process what he had said about **Understanding, Respect, and Trust**. All of this was too much and they sat there speechless.

Finally, Alisha spoke up, "I guess we have to go back to the drawing board! We need to spend some time rethinking what you've told us and try to think about things from a spiritual not just a human perspective. I'm not even sure how to do that! Where do we start?"

Cole in his normal confused state spoke up, "I'm not even sure we can get there from here. We may have to go somewhere else to start!"

"I have all the confidence in the world in you two!" bragged W.G. "I think you will begin to get the hang of it if you just go back to the beginning and answer one simple question." He paused and looked at the couple. They both sat there with that look on their face like, "Duh, what is the one question?" W.G. continued, "What is it that you really SEEK?" And, as was his custom, he was gone!

Cole and Alisha decided they would begin their search for that answer by each taking some time to think about the "One Question" individually and then sit down and compare notes. Each of them got a composition book to record their thoughts so they would be able to more clearly express themselves as they contemplated this incredibly complex idea.

A few days later, when they sat down to discuss their thoughts, they were amazed at how similar their thought processes were. They each concluded that they began with a bunch of disjointed thoughts that made absolutely no sense. Cole had even written down: THIS IS STUPID! IT'S GETTING ME NOWHERE! when he first began recording his thoughts. Both agreed that the more they wrote and reread what they wrote, their thinking became clearer and more succinct.

Cole shared that he realized his thought process always centered on how Alisha's actions and reactions impacted him—how they made him feel. He seemed to think that he was the cultural center of the universe and everything was supposed to comply with his idea of right and wrong, his concept of happiness. He thought back to his discussion with Ben and Don about how to get everyone on the same page. He reflected on how Ben had told him that was the wrong question because everyone was already on the same page and the page read, *I'm right and you're wrong. The world would be a much better place if you would just see things my way!"*

Alisha laughed when he shared that with her. Then she sheepishly agreed that her thoughts had been along much the same line. After much discussion they concluded the objective of an intentional relationship was for each to SEEK to make the other happy and feel understood, respected, and trusted. In other words, to make each other feel loved!

Feeling really good about the discussion they had and the conclusion they had come to, they began to wonder where to go and what to do next. When would W.G. get back to them and move on to the next building block? They felt somewhat lost since they had no address, phone number, email address, or social media account by which to reach him. They didn't know when or where or even in what form they would see him again. He did say, "I'll meet with you each week." That was comforting but only slightly!

All week they worked diligently at applying their new understanding of **Understanding, Respect, and Trust**. Sometimes they were more successful than others. Sometimes they failed miserably! Each time they failed they were quick to point it out to each other. One day while they were in an intense discussion (that's what they called it!), each calling the other's attention to the mistakes they had made, there was a knock on the door. Cole stopped his critical review of Alisha long enough to answer the door.

It was the delivery boy again! This time the envelope contained a card for each of them. Except for the name on the card, each read the same. The front read:

**God grant me the serenity to except
the people I cannot change,**

the courage to change the people I can,

and the wisdom to know

It's me!

The back of each card read:

Spiritual Pattern and Principle # 4:

It "IS" about you. "THEY" are NOT the problem.

Embarrassed by the frankness and timeliness of the message, they realized he obviously knew the direction their conversation had taken. Reluctantly, they retreated from their critical positions. They agreed that, at this point in their quest, it was not a good idea for each to critique the other. For the remainder of the week, they decided they would each focus their critical attention on themselves.

Friday rolled around and they were beginning to wonder when W.G. would contact them next. He didn't say anything on the last card about when they should meet again. Their first encounter, just two weeks before, had been pretty clear cut. Last week was a little freaky with the surprise appearance at the coffee shop. Both had been on Saturday, so they assumed that they would see him again tomorrow.

Alisha's car needed to be serviced, so after breakfast they dropped her car off at the shop so she could take Cole to work and use his car for the day. They arranged to have Alisha's mom pick the kids up at school so they would already be taken care of. They would use tonight to discuss the events of the week and to prepare their explanation of the week's ups and downs to W.G. when he showed up tomorrow.

Alisha arrived at Cole's office right on time. They headed to the auto shop to pick up her car. As they stopped at the traffic light just before reaching the shop a young man approached their car. Cole thought, *Another bum looking for drug money!* He looked like a typical teenager. He was dressed in jeans and a hoodie. He wore sneakers and the waist band of his pants was down around mid-thigh and his plaid underwear was showing. *How could any-one think that is cool? How can you walk down the street holding your pants up with one hand?* Cole thought. "Quick, roll up your window and don't look him in the eye. Maybe he'll go away!" he called to Alisha. The young man had a spray bottle and a rag in his hand. He leaned over their car hood and quickly sprayed the windshield, wiped it clean, smiled, said, "God Bless," and walked away.

They were both astonished. "What was that all about?" Cole lamented. Then he noticed a piece of paper stuck under the windshield wiper. *What is that he left on our windshield, some kind of advertise-ment?*" he thought. When they got to the auto repair shop, he reached for the piece of paper and tossed it to Alisha while he attended to the matter of her car with the shop attendant.

While Alisha waited for Cole, she turned the card over and noticed the same beautiful print. The envelope read: THINGS AREN'T ALWAYS WHAT THEY SEEM! and the card inside read: MEET ME AT THE COFFEE SHOP IN AN HOUR. It was signed W.G. Atap.

They were both a little flustered. They had each counted on having the night to talk about the week's events and prepare for their meeting. Now they barely had time to take Alisha's car home and make it back to the coffee shop by the appointed time.

CHAPTER 16

COMMUNICATION COMES IN THREE STYLES

As they approached the coffee shop, Alisha was bothered by the fact she had no opportunity to change her clothes and touch up her makeup. Cole was just bothered! There at the corner table sat W.G. This time he had no ragamuffins with him, just his raggedy self, holding court as if he was king of the world.

Cole immediately began his cross examination, "Why the sudden meeting? Just suppose we had not already sent the kids to their grandmother's? How are we to know when you are going to call these impromptu meetings? Why couldn't you have given us a little advanced notice?"

W.G. looked at him with those penetrating eyes and calmly said, "I suppose you still think this is all a coincidence. Just like the man on the street corner, the 'ragamuffins,' as you so affectionately refer to them, the delivery boy, and the teenager who summoned you for me! It never ceases to amaze me how you humans refer to things that are beyond your finite understanding as 'coincidence' or 'circumstances' or, my all-time favorite, 'a situation'!" The things that happen outside your scope of rationale are not merely coincidental. Let me assure you there are no coincidences! Whatever 'circumstance' you find yourself in is exactly where you are supposed to be! The real question is, when you find yourself there, are you willing to allow for the possibility that there is something to be learned from that 'situation,' 'circumstance,' or 'coincidence?' Or do you immediately begin your pity party, with 'poor pitiful me,' 'ain't it awful,' or again, my personal favorite, 'Why me, Lord?' I say, 'Why not you!' Everything that happens, happens for a reason. Sometimes it is to make you stronger. Sometimes it's to teach you something. At other times it is intended simply to help you understand that you aren't the center of the universe! And occasionally, you will not understand the event until long after the experience has passed, maybe months or even years later. Either way, I will let you in on a little secret! My favorite spiritual pattern and principle is #11." He pulled out a couple of cards and handed one to each of them. On the cards, in the same beautiful print to which they had grown accustomed, was written: **Spiritual Pattern and Principle #11:** *You are every bit as smart as you think you are, but you don't know as much as you think you know!* "Put these in your wallet or purse so you will have ready access to them at critical times," he said. "I think you will find this one particularly useful as we begin to tackle building block #2: **Communication comes in three styles**.

They both looked at him as if he were speaking Greek or something. It was Cole, once again, who broke the silence. In his typical defensive manner he said, "Now, wait just a minute. If we have anything going for us, it's communication. We talk to each other all the time. We don't sit in silence or shut each other out like many of our friends. You can't hang that one on us!" He looked at W.G. as if to say, "Gotcha!" Alisha was nodding approvingly as Cole attempted to exonerate them.

"That's great!" exclaimed The Teacher. "What is Alisha's favorite color? What is it that she wants most out of life? And Alisha, what is Cole's greatest fear? What does he want most out of life?"

They both looked at each other and back at him with that 'deer in the headlights' look. "Busted!" Cole confessed. "What are you trying to say?" he begged.

"I'm referring to the quality of your communication," he responded. "Communication actually comes in three styles: casual, conflict, and committed. Let me explain. Most people spend the vast majority of their lives engaged in casual communication. They talk about the weather, entertainment, sports, the neighbors, or (once again my all-time favorite) politics. They talk about things that are safe and nonthreatening, things that reveal little or nothing about who they truly are and what they feel deeply about. They don't want to risk being made fun of or being taken too seriously. They surely don't want to let down their guard and have others, even those closest to them, find out about their weaknesses, their fears, or their failures. It's because of this that most marriage counselors will tell you lack of communication is one of the most common causes of the breakdown of the marriage relationship. Husbands and wives talk but they don't really say anything. They don't know each other even after years of marriage."

He paused for a minute to let that sink in. Then he continued. "The second style of communication is what I call conflict."

"Hold it right there," Cole jumped in again. "You can't pin that one on us. We have our share of conflict. I'm always telling her she just doesn't get it and she tells me I'm stubborn or not listening to her. We always kiss and make up, but we certainly have our share of conflict," he said proudly. Alisha looked at him as if she wished she could crawl under the table. Or more like she wished he'd crawl under the table!

"That is true!" The Teacher continued. "But that's not what I'm talking about. You see, I'm referring to intentional, positive, and productive conflict. It's conflict that couples avoid at all costs because they have not taken the time to build the **Understanding, Respect, and Trust** that would allow them to talk freely about the things that bother them most without starting World War III. This is a process and not an event. It takes time, effort, and intentionality. That's why you can't get this from a book or a DVD or a weekend retreat. It takes time in the flight simulator. It's practice, critique, practice, critique, then practice some more until these skills become second nature to each of you. It happens over time. There are no shortcuts."

"Only after you have begun to achieve this level of **Understanding, Respect, and Trust** can you then begin to intentionally introduce **Conflict** into your lives and expect to have a positive outcome," he continued. "Then, and only then, can you begin to talk about why you have to go to her mother's house again this weekend or why he gets to spend another weekend at the golf course while you're stuck at home with the kids. Only then can you begin to help each other understand the little things that get under your skin and talk about mistakes, fears, and failures in a way that will allow you both to grow instead of fight and pout or revert to the silent treatment which never accomplishes anything! I call this the ability to cuss, fuss, and discuss. Of course, that's just an expression. I don't really mean for you to cuss!" he said with a chuckle. "Does this make any sense to you?"

Simultaneously they shouted, "Ouch, that hurts!" You know, like the dog that gets hit by the stick thrown into the pack and lets everyone else know he's the guilty dog! "I hear what you're saying," Cole confessed. "She is always telling me, 'It's not what you say but how you say it!' I am guilty as charged. How do I get over that terrible habit?"

"Count me in!" Alisha added with gusto. "I'm guilty too!"

"Well," W.G. continued, "let's talk a little about the 'WHY' and then I'll share more about the 'HOW TO.' It is only after you spend the time, effort, and energy to intentionally develop **Understanding, Respect, and Trust** that you will be able to intentionally introduce conflict into your communication and be able to discuss it without going to war. You will be able to help each other overcome your shortfalls and learn from your mistakes instead of living in that competitive 'I'm right and you're wrong' mode. You will be amazed at how much deeper your relationship will develop and how you'll be able to make decisions faster and accomplish more without all the anger and residual feelings that once resulted from conflict. This is what I call the third style: committed communication. It's when you are able to bring up the subjects that you normally avoid at all cost. When you can talk about them without getting defensive or feeling the need to show your spouse how smart you are and how dumb they are! Does that sound like something you'd be interested in?" he asked.

Again, Cole replied with the finesse of a bull in a china shop, "Is that a rhetorical question? Of course, we want that!"

Although she was embarrassed by her husband's lack of tact, Alisha nodded in agreement. "Yes, how do we get that?" she implored.

"OK, then! Here are a couple of flight simulator exercises I want you to practice this week.

<u>First:</u> As you find yourselves getting agitated with each other this week, I want you to focus on your own feelings and not on the action or reaction from your spouse. Ask yourself, 'Where is that feeling coming from?' 'Is this from some unrealistic or self-centered expectation I have imposed on my mate?' Resist the temptation to point out their grave mistake. Focus on your feelings!

<u>Second:</u> When you notice your mate is bewildered, frustrated, angry, or otherwise in a state of agitation, ask yourself, 'Did I say or do something that showed a lack of **Understanding, Respect, or Trust** that could have led to his or her not feeling loved by me?

As you progress through the week, write your observations in your journal. This is not for the purpose of later convicting you of your egregious acts of insensitivity. Rather, it is to help you focus on self-correction and self-improvement. Can you do that?"

Reluctantly at first and then with a great deal more enthusiasm, they both nodded and agreed to spend time in the flight simulator this week. "How much time do I need to spend on this?" Cole asked.

"I find it amusing that you humans always want to know how many questions you can miss and still pass the test. It is entirely up to you! How much time you spend depends on how much you want to achieve this level of intentional relationship with your wife!" W.G. said. "For example, let's say that you decide as a couple that you want to retire at age fifty-seven with a million dollars in your portfolio. If you spend five minutes per week thinking about and discussing your options and making investment decisions, how is that going to work out for your?"

"OK, I get your point!" Cole chimed in. "I know, 'you get out what you put in'!" Alisha rolled her eyes and looked at W.G. as if to say, 'What is a girl to do? What chance do I have? Look at what I have to work with!'

"Great!" W.G. said with a belly laugh. In that instant he was gone, leaving Cole and Alisha staring at each other in bewilderment but with a glimmer of hope and excitement about the prospects of enjoying this kind of marriage relationship in the near future.

On the way home, they experienced a little sample that let them know this week would be one for the record books. Cole was known to drive with what Alisha affectionately called reckless abandon. He drove a bit too fast and a little too close to the vehicles ahead. Alisha was known do a little of what Cole affectionately called backseat driving. On more than one occasion during the fifteen-minute drive home they caught themselves falling back into the "let me tell you how it's done" mode. It happened so many times in that short distance they actually broke out laughing at their natural inclination to criticize each other. By the end of the week, they were more than ready for another therapy session with The Teacher.

CHAPTER 17

YOU'RE NOT THE BOSS OF ME
(OR ARE YOU?)

During the week they had been through so many teachable moments they didn't know if they were coming or going. However, they did get an occasional glimpse of what it felt like when each was fully aware of how what they said and did affected the other. When they were "in the zone" and focused on making the other feel loved, they clearly felt a difference. They felt more connected to each other, more a part of each other. Those fleeting moments were incredible! So much so, they knew they wanted to continue their practice sessions until this became a way of life instead of the serendipitous occurrence.

Saturday they were up early. They ate and rushed the kids off to grandmother's house so they could get to the coffee shop. They still didn't know how but they realized that when they showed up, W.G. would be there. He just seemed to show up at the precise moment they needed him most.

When they arrived, he was sitting in a booth in the rear. "Well, how did it go?" he asked, as if he didn't already know! They both began to rattle on like school children on the playground. On and on they went about how they would be engaged in some intense conversation about which of them had screwed up. Then, like something whacked them on the side of their head, they would realize what they were doing to each other. They would come back to the practice session and focus on making each other feel loved and things would level off. They were absolutely amazed at the difference in their relationship when each was focused on the other and not themselves.

"It just seems like so much work for these brief glimpses of happiness!" Cole blurted. "Why can't we enjoy this all the time? It doesn't seem fair!"

"I'm sorry, Cole" said The Teacher. "Maybe I should have explained that this is a process. It happens slowly, bit by bit with practice, practice, practice over time. There are no shortcuts. That's why I call it a process and not an event!" Alisha looked at The Teacher with that 'What can I say!' look.

Cole knew he'd been busted again. "I guess I'm just a little slow on the uptake," he replied in a child-like tone. "You're going to have to remember that as you begin to work on building block #3," W.G. said, looking directly at Cole as if to say, "Read my lips! This is important. This will be on the test!" He reached into his pocket and gave them each another card. They read: Building Block #3: **Responsibility, you're not the boss of me (or are you?).**

This time they both had that "Have we just landed on planet Zenon!" look. "I know," said W.G. "We're going to have to spend a little time on this one before I turn you loose on each other. The focus on building block #3 is Responsibility. I need you to **change the way you think** about responsibility. In your mind, responsibility is about power, control, and authority. In a small way that's true. However, it's not about power over or control of each other but of yourself and the impact you have on the other. That's why you first have to spend time building **Understanding, Respect, and Trust** so you can develop the ability to 'Cuss, Fuss, and Discuss' moving from **Casual through Conflict to Committed Communication** in order to develop **Responsibility**. Your responsibility is both to each other and for each other but not over each other. You need to think about what your responsibility is to your wife when you 'SAY' you want a deeper relationship, but you spend every weekend with your buddies on the golf course. What is your responsibility to your husband when you 'SAY' I love you, but you give every minute of you time, energy, and attention to the house, the kids, the school, the church, and the community—to everybody but him? Ask yourself, 'How will what I'm about to say or do make him or her feel? Will it convey that I love them or will it convey that I think I'm superior to them or that I think they should be happy that I still have them ranked in the top ten?' Cole, she is not responsible for your happiness, you are! Alisha, he is not responsible for your happiness, you are! But both of you are responsible to each other as helpmates."

"Now that's not fair!" rebutted Cole. "I don't try to boss her around. She is her own woman and I am my own man. We are not that way!" He looked at them both as if he expected to get a gold star and smiley face for his discourse.

"Cole, Cole, Cole," W.G. said with a note of exasperation. "You remind me so much of a fisherman I once knew. So bold, so brash, so out of touch! I'm not talking about being bossy but about realizing what power your thoughts, actions, and reactions have over your spouse's feelings of self-worth. It's not the bossiness as much as the little things you do. When you roll your eyes as if to say, 'You're so stupid' or when you walk out on a conversation that makes you uncomfortable, leaving your mate feeling disconnected, unloved, and not cared for. When you say things like, 'There you go again,' or 'See, I told you this would happen,' or you make little jokes to your friends about your spouse. You make them feel less loved, less of a human being, less important. That's what I mean about being responsible to and for each other. That's when you realize you are, in fact, the boss of each other and that is a tremendous burden or a tremendous honor. And that, my friend, depends entirely on how you choose to accept and carry out that responsibility."

"Wow, I never thought of it that way," they both exclaimed out loud.

"You think?" W.G. replied to their lament. "That's why pattern and principle #1 is **Change the way you think about the things you think about**!

These are not individual items to be memorized so you can regurgitate them at test time. They are skills to be learned and applied. They're interconnected and totally integrated into the process of being intentional. They grow out of and lead into each other. They need to become, not academic, but a way of life if you want to develop the relationship you SAY you SEEK."

"The more I understand the more inadequate I feel," Cole said. "I'm not sure I'll ever get this right! I'm such a screw up! It's hopeless!"

"That's my boy!" laughed W.G. "I have good news for you. Everybody I've ever been able to lead to greatness over the ages was first, as you say, 'a screw up'! That's when they know that what they finally are able to accomplish didn't come from them but from a higher power outside themselves. You are finally getting it! Remember pattern and principle #7: **You'll never be perfect, but that's no excuse not to try and get better.** That is exactly where you are, my boy. You are at the beginning of the two steps forward and one step back process. You are on the edge of discovery and are wondering whether or not to take that next step. If you are willing to quit looking for the quick fix and understand the process, you will begin to experience a level of abundant living beyond your wildest imagination. It will simply surpass all understanding! But you first have to get out of your own way. Stop trying to understand it or figure it out or explain it in rational terms and let the process I've given you work. Can you do that?"

"I'll certainly try. Lord only knows I want what you've been talking about!" Cole replied.

"Yes, I do!" W.G. said with a little grin. "Here is your flight simulator exercise for the week," he continued. "I want you to intentionally set aside fifteen minutes for an appointment with each other this week to sit and talk about what the relationship you desire with each other would look like, sound like, and feel like. What is it that you really SEEK? Let me caution you! Don't get involved in critiquing each other's thoughts. Don't get caught up in the 'my dog's bigger than your dog syndrome. It's not about whose idea is biggest or best. It's about sharing your dreams and hopes for the future. It will feel awkward at first. You'll feel like you're spinning your wheels and getting nowhere. Trust me, if you work the process, you will begin to get a better idea of what success in your relationship would look like. Until you get a clear picture in your mind of what that looks like, you simply cannot plot a course to reach that destination. I want each of you to write your observations in your journal and we'll get together again next week to talk about your progress and where to go from here."

This time it was Alisha who broke the silence. "Every time he does that, it freaks me out! I'll never get use to his vanishing act," she continued. "I know," Cole joined in. "I know!" With that, they headed home to begin the practice they both knew they needed so desperately.

"This is going to be a tough week for me," exclaimed Cole. "We have several closings to work through and our company is hosting the annual meeting for realtors for the entire state on Friday. I'm just not sure when I'll have time!" "Me too!" Alisha chimed in. "I have parent teacher conferences with both the kids' schools. Taylor has her basketball tournament starting next week. Alex has tryouts for the baseball team, and you know how important that is. I haven't had time to have lunch with the girls in weeks, and I just don't know when I'll find time either!"

As they walked up the walkway and reached for the door knob, they saw a familiar looking envelope taped to the front door. You guessed it, written in beautiful print! They tore it open to find another card that read: IF YOU WANT YOUR DREAMS TO COME TRUE, YOU MUST NOT OVERSLEEP! YOU WILL NEVER "FIND" THE TIME TO MAKE YOUR DREAMS COME TRUE. YOU HAVE TO "MAKE" IT!

"How does he do that?" Cole clamored. "OK," they both said. "Let's sit down right now and make the time to do this before we meet with him next week." It took some finagling and some schedule adjustments, but they finally carved out fifteen minutes to sit down and talk about where they wanted their relationship to go. They would send the kids to grandma's Thursday night.

When they finally got around to the appointed time, they had both already made a few notes about what they thought the intentional relationship would look like. "In the perfect relationship," Cole started, "I would spend more time with you and the kids. I would focus more on making sure you know how much you mean to me by the things I do as well as what I say. I would give more thought to how the things I say and do would make you feel. I wouldn't spend so much time critiquing and spend more time choosing to relish the qualities in you that attracted me to you in the first place."

Alisha jumped in with her thoughts. "I would spend less time worrying about how neatly detailed everything is around the house. I'd give less time to outside interests that really don't do anything to enhance our relationship. I'd probably adjust my idea of what 'perfect' should be and choose to appreciate what we have instead of continually thinking about what we don't have. I'd spend more time letting you know what I enjoy and appreciate about you instead of critiquing the things I think you should change to meet my preconceived expectations."

Almost simultaneously they began to laugh. They both realized that when they began writing down their thoughts they started with all the things they would change about the other. But as they read their thoughts and rewrote them they began to realize the need to change their focus. Now their thoughts centered on changes they needed to make in themselves to have the desired impact on the other. They truly had begun to grasp spiritual pattern and principle #5: It "IS" about you. "THEY" are the NOT problem.

The excitement about their progress was overwhelming. They wished they had some way to contact The Teacher so they could share their newfound awareness. "Why doesn't he give us a number or something so we can reach him when we need him?" Cole bemoaned. "This waiting for him to show up is for the birds!" As he was blabbering on and on about how inconvenient it was to get in touch with W.G., he noticed another envelope lying on the table. It was right there in front of them. How had they not seen it when they were sharing their thoughts from their journals? He grabbed it and ripped it open. The message read: **Ask and you will receive, knock and the door will be opened!** "Oh, that's cute, real cute. Now we're back to vacation Bible school stories. What's next? Are we going to hear about how Zacchaeus was a wee little man and then sing Kumbaya?"

Just as he paused his critical tirade, there was a knock at the door. "I did it again, didn't I!" Cole cried. "It's him, isn't it? You get the door while I find a hole to crawl into," he continued.

Alisha opened the door and said apologetically, "He really is trying!"

Cole began his much overdue apology as, "I'm sorry, I was in the other room getting both feet out of my mouth! When will I ever learn?"

"That's OK," replied W.G. "Some of you are just slower learners than others!"

They all got a good laugh out of that, but Cole felt like he was about two inches tall. He wished he could learn that every thought that enters his mind doesn't have to come out of his mouth. "I don't get my feelings hurt easily," added W.G. "That's why I only require faith the size of a mustard seed. I can work with the smallest of minds!" Again he chuckled. He suggested they go back in the kitchen, which seemed like the place people preferred to talk about serious issues.

CHAPTER 18

ACCOUNTABILITY AND ACTION

After the embarrassment dissipated, the couple began to share quite enthusiastically their newfound truths. They went on and on about how they had begun to **Change the way they think about the things they think about**. They both spoke of how they now were focused on the changes they needed to make in themselves instead of the other. They shared some of the desired changes they had previously discussed. The most interesting observation was the fact that they were so surprised at the positive outcome. They were amazed at how more connected they felt to each other.

"I'm pleased that you have decided to spend more time in the flight simulator," W.G. added. "You will find the more you focus on the spiritual truths in the patterns and principles and the more you utilize the five building blocks, the more you will experience feelings of oneness, meaning, and inner happiness. That is the idea behind two becoming one. That was the plan all along!"

"Let's continue our foray into the five building blocks," he continued as he handed each of them another card which read: **Building Block #5: Accountability**.

"This one seems pretty cut and dried. I know I am accountable for my part and she is accountable for her part. Relationships are a 50/50 proposition, right?" Cole interrupted. The look on his face indicated he fully expected extra points for his wisdom. The look on Alisha's face indicated otherwise!

"It's a little more complicated than that," replied W.G. "It's not so much about each of you doing your 'fair share.' It is more about how you have developed your relationship in order to respond to each other when you haven't done your fair share. And, at times, realizing that each will have to do more than their fair share." This time both Cole and Alisha had that "I don't understand" expression on their faces. "Let me explain," he said, trying to remove that lost in space feeling that gripped the couple. "The understanding of **Accountability** in this context is contingent upon your spending sufficient time, effort, and energy on the other three building blocks. This will help you to understand and utilize this much misunderstood one. In other words, you must first properly develop **Understanding, Respect, and Trust**. Then you will be able to engage in deeper **Communication**. That will enable you to work through conflict and get to committed communication without all the residual feelings that normally accompany conflict. Once you learn to do that, you are then able to share **Responsibility** both to each other and for each other. When you have properly learned to apply these first three, you are then, and only then, ready to hold each other **Accountable**. That means when you both agree to a certain plan of action and one of you fails to deliver, you not only have given the other partner the right but also the responsibility to come and talk to you about that short fall. This is the trickiest of the five! If you haven't properly applied the first three before you begin to utilize this one, the wheels can really begin to come off!"

"Let me illustrate. We'll go back to the financial example since it's so easy to measure success or failure. Again, let's say you've agreed you want to retire at age fifty-seven with a million dollars in your portfolio. In order to do so you both agree to a budget that requires you to be frugal. (You've heard of a budget, right?) Then when your annual review at work is completed and you get that much anticipated raise, Cole comes home with a new set of golf clubs. This is clearly outside the agreed upon budget. In which case Cole should fully expect Alisha to approach him and say, 'Remember our retirement goals? We need to talk.' Or if Alisha comes home with a new $300 purse, she should expect the same response from Cole. If you have properly learned to apply the first three building blocks, you can have this **Accountability** conversation without starting World War III or name calling or any number of nonproductive reactions that, otherwise, will occur. You can do this without the residual feelings because you **Understand, Respect, and Trust** each other. You are able to engage in a positive intentional **Conflicted** conversation about the purchase that doesn't match up with the agreed upon retirement plan. Then you can move to **Committed Communication** that allows you to be **Responsible** to and for each other.

"That sounds so simple!" replied Cole. "I'd love to live in that world but, WOW, is that hard to deliver? Do couples really live like that or does that only happen on Zenon or wherever you're from?" he added with exasperation.

Alisha added, "I should only wish to live in that world!"

"It is not only possible, it is promised. It's called abundant living and it applies to the here and now as well as the hereafter. The difference between those two is, in the hereafter you simply have to accept the Creator God's plan of salvation. You can't work for it or earn it! In the here and now you can only enjoy abundant living by intentionally learning and applying the spiritual patterns and principles and building blocks to your daily lives. The degree of abundance you receive in the here and now is directly proportional to the effort you put into applying those spiritual truths. You get out what you put in! Remember, we talked about the effort required. If you spend five minutes per week planning for your retirement goals, you are not likely to be very successful. The more effort and energy you put into it, the more likely you are to reach your goals. It's about pattern and principle #5: **What you 'SEEK' is more important than what you 'SAY.'** Can you follow that line of thinking?" He paused to look at the couple as if to say, "Work with me here!"

Although they were a little numb from the information overload, they were equally excited about the prospect and the promise of what The Teacher was revealing to them. He spoke with such authority they actually believed it was possible. "We believe you," they both exclaimed, "but how can we ever do that? It just seems so hard!"

"You've already taken the first and most important step," he answered. "Once you move from doubt to belief that it can actually take place, you are on your way. You must remember, though, as you have already discovered in spiritual pattern and principle #6: **It's simple but it is not easy, you must spend time in the flight simulator**, it must become a way of life if you want to reach your desired goals in life."

With that, he pulled out another of the familiar cards. It read: **Building Block #5: Action leads to results!**

After sticking his foot in his mouth so many times Cole was now smarter than the average bear. He commented, almost requesting permission to speak, "That really sounds like a no brainer! That's the number one rule of business. I do know a little bit about that." He then waited for W.G. or Alisha to put him in his place.

"That is true," W.G. replied. "That is the number one rule in business, but this is not business, it's life. That's why **Action** is the fifth building block instead of the first. The first four prepare you to properly and powerfully utilize number five. Without the proper preparation you will spin your wheels and never reach the results you desire. You see, in the application of the spiritual patterns and principles, everything produces after its own kind. Positive thoughts produce positive actions and reactions which in turn produce positive results. Likewise, negative thinking produces negative actions and re-actions resulting in negative outcomes. It can be no other way. You choose every day, by the actions and reactions you take, what the results will be. When you choose to pick at your mate and focus on the things you don't like, you choose to be unhappy. She doesn't make you unhappy, you choose that path. When you choose to act and react to circumstances as if they can be overcome, they will be. If you choose to wallow in self-pity and play 'ain't it awful' that life has dealt me a bad hand, then your life will be just as miserable as you imagine it to be."

"That sure sounds a lot like new age to me. I've read those books and tried closing my eyes and click-ing my heels three times and wishing I was back in Kansas or somewhere over the rainbow, and it just doesn't work that way," Cole blurted out again.

Alisha thought, *If you keep sticking your neck out there with those harebrained statements, you're going to end up in Kansas!*

The old man smiled at Alisha as if to say, "I know, I know!" Then he turned to Cole. "If you remember, Ben and Don told you this is not new age. This is not about black magic or even mind control. It's about HEART control. Your heart is that part of you that is created in the image of the Creator God. It's your inner being, not just your mind. However, your mind is the key tool in helping you open your heart to the concept of becoming the 'you' God intended. It's that part of you where no one knows what's going on but you and God. When you choose to think, act, and react with faith, hope, love, and forgiveness in your heart, you begin to move toward abundant living. In order to do this, you first have to get your limited intellectual understanding of how the world works out of your way. Then you can begin to think, act, and react with a spiritual understanding of how the world works. I think you will find that the world will respond to you in a manner well beyond your wildest dreams when you let this change take place in your heart.

Let me give you another example. Let's say God changed His mind and gave you permission not to love everybody (which, by the way, God never will. God never changes! That's why God is God and you are not!), but let's say He did allow you to have just one person you didn't have to love. Most people already have that person picked out! I can tell you have one picked out by the look on your face! Well, that's one place He wants you to start **Changing the way you think about the things you think about**. Begin to think of that person as having been created in God's image. When you look at them try to see the face of God. How would your thoughts, actions, and reactions to them be different?"

"Man, am I slow!" Cole replied.

"You're not alone. There's a lot of that going on!" responded W.G. "The important thing is you are beginning to realize that you are your own worst enemy. Quit trying to make things that are well beyond your comprehension fit into your neat little picture of how the world works. Quit leaning on your own understanding. Acknowledge that the Creator God is who He says He is and He has your best interest at heart. Trust in his spiritual patterns and principles and your path will become clear and your life abundant."

"OK, I want to get out of the way and let God's spiritual patterns and principles guide my life. What can I do to get there? How do I make this happen?" Cole begged.

Alisha was nodding her head enthusiastically. "Yes, what do we do now?" she added.

"I want you both to spend some serious time in the flight simulator," W.G. began. "Be intentional and protective about your quest. Set a specific time for the two of you to go back and review our original question, 'What do you really want out of life?' Write your thoughts on a life planning chart. Focus on what you REALLY want in these six areas of life: 1. Spiritual, 2. Physical, 3. Financial, 4. Personal/Family and Friends, 5. Professional/Career, and 6. Community/Giving Back. Be cautious of the many things that will pull at your attention and try to disrupt your focus. Things that seem important at the time but really could be eliminated or placed at a lower priority than life planning. When you find yourself getting caught up in the busyness of day-to-day life, go to the bathroom mirror and look yourself in the eye and say out loud, 'I'm too busy to plan my life!' I want you to think about the foolishness of that statement. Yet, most humans fall into that category. They are just too busy to take control of their own life so they let the chips fall where they may and then they blame me for the life they get. Don't let this happen to you! You will, in fact, never FIND the time to plan your life. You have to MAKE the time! There are no shortcuts. Make the commitment to learn to live intentionally!"

Once again, the couple found themselves alone staring at each other across the table. "What now? Do we just go home and keep on keeping on?" Cole asked.

"I guess the ball is in our court now," Alisha responded. "He said we need to spend some serious time contemplating what we really want out of life. I assume that means we need to do some life planning. We need to get more specific about what we want. It's more than just being happy or successful." They headed home a little overwhelmed but with a commitment to begin to live intentionally. When they arrived home, they fell onto the couch to recover from the intense session they had just experienced.

As they sat there, Cole had a few disconcerting thoughts. *Is that all there is? Is he through with us? Will we ever see him again? What if we have questions?* He was beginning to feel a major panic attack coming on. He then noticed something on the mantle. It was a large manila envelope standing upright against the bookends next to his Bible. On the front of the envelope written, in the familiar beautiful print, was **Fear not, I will never leave you.** Inside was a note and six life planning forms, one for each of the six areas The Teacher had mentioned. The note read: START HERE. PERHAPS THESE WILL HELP RELIEVE SOME OF THE PANIC YOU MUST BE FEELING RIGHT NOW! IT WAS SIGNED, FOREVER YOURS, W.G.

Over the next few months, they made time to get away from the hustle and bustle for some serious life planning. They continued to pray together as a couple. They regularly asked the Creator God for guidance. At first these actions seemed to be foreign to them. But the more they practiced the more natural they felt.

They even went to their favorite resort in Gatlinburg, Tennessee, and spent the weekend admiring God's handiwork, walking and talking about what they REALLY wanted out of life. They would make notes as they talked about each of the six areas of life. Just as they experienced with their first attempt at keeping a journal, their early notes made little sense. Some of them were even bordering on ridiculous. For example: "Physical – *To look and feel like we did at 25* and, Financial – *To die rich!*"

As they continued to talk and write down their thoughts, they noticed their thoughts became clearer and some more specific goals began to emerge from the fog in their brains. Finally, what began as chaos, with no visible way of ever making sense, much less making a difference, began to take shape. They began to realize that by intentionally talking about and thinking about what they REALLY wanted they began to draw a picture of what success and happiness would look like and feel like in their ideal world. Slowly but surely, they began to work together on their plan. Sometimes things came together just as they planned, but most often it didn't work out exactly like they envisioned. They frequently found themselves going back to the drawing board to clarify or even redefine one or more areas of their life plan.

What surprised them even more than the success with which they were beginning to achieve some of their initial goals was the way they were able to hold each other accountable when one failed to deliver on their agreed upon responsibilities. They knew when they fell short that the other would say, "We need to talk." More importantly, this did not result in arguments, as it did before. Now they had learned to **Understand, Respect, and Trust** that when they attempted to hold each other accountable it was not to be judgmental or out of feelings of competitive superiority. Now they knew the accountability was out of genuine care and concern for each other's well-being.

They did not find themselves living in the land of make believe. Cole still got on her nerves now and then and Alisha still irritated him when he was focused on his little world and she would interrupt. However, they did find that their little irritations occurred less often and seemed to be less intense. Many of the things that once bothered them didn't seem so important now.

CHAPTER 19

WHAT, IN THE WORLD, ARE YOU GOING TO DO?

The girls could contain themselves no longer! One day while having lunch they both blurted out, "What about the affair? You caught him, didn't you? Who is it? Do you have pictures? That's why you two are all 'lovey-dovey' now, isn't it? You think we don't notice? Well, we do and it's time you give us the dirt."

The moment of truth had come! Alisha had been dreading this moment since she and Cole had the encounter with Ben and Don in Justin's office. "What will I say? I can't tell them about angels and a mysterious teacher who just shows up occasionally, for Pete's sake!" Silently, she was pouring over the litany of fearful outcomes that could result from this conversation. At that precise moment she glanced out the window of the restaurant and noticed a car driving by. In the driver's seat was, you guessed it, Don, with Ben in the passenger seat and, none other in the backseat but their friend, Andre.

All three looked her in the eye, winked, and smiled as if to say, "We've got your back!" As they drove away, she felt a sense of calm as she began to explain to her friends that she and Cole had come to realize that there was more to their relationship than they were experiencing and that they had, through very special friends, been introduced to some spiritual patterns and principles that would lead them to an intentional relationship with God and each other. She continued to tell them about how they had begun to seek the relationship that the Creator God had intended for every relationship and the difference it had made in theirs.

The girls sat spellbound as Alisha continued talking about what they had experienced and how their relationship was so much more meaningful now than it had ever been. There was no doubt that this was a different Alisha than the girls knew just a few months ago.

As the waiter came to take their drink order, Nina said, "I'll have what she's having!" They all had a good laugh, but now a different seed had been planted. Instead of the seeds of fear, distrust, and despair being planted in Alisha's mind, this time it was Alisha planting the seed of hope and possibility in the minds of Julie and Nina.

Alisha couldn't wait for Cole to pick her up so she could share the experience. He burst out in laughter when she told him about Ben, Don, and Andre making an appearance at just the right moment. "That is just how I would expect them to roll!" he bellowed.

"You know," she exclaimed somewhat in surprise, "it has given me an opportunity to share with them some of the spiritual patterns and principles. They genuinely see a difference in our lives and want to experience what we are beginning to experience. I'm enjoying our sharing sessions, and they seem to be eager to learn more about being intentional in their own relationships."

"That's wild," he replied. "That's the last response I would have ever expected from those two. Will wonders never cease? But, now that I think about it," he changed pace, "Austin has been asking some questions too. We've had a couple of conversations about the spiritual patterns and principles and intentional building blocks. He too seems to have noticed a change in us and is genuinely interested in how we did it!"

Just as he was beginning to expound on his evaluation of Alisha's friends, there was a knock at the door. Alex ran to the door and threw it open. He did this despite what his mom had told him a million times, without giving thought to whether it might be Jack the Ripper or some serial killer looking for his next victim. "Mom, it's the mailman!" Alex yelled from the door. Alisha went to the door to apologize for her son's irresponsibility. Standing there with a familiar manila envelope in his hands was Bobby, the mailman again!

"Sorry to stop by so late," he said, "but this was in the bottom of my mail bag when I finished my route. I don't remember putting it in there this morning when I prepared for the day, but it looks important so I thought I'd bring it by." Alisha thanked him for going the extra mile and again apologized for Alex's capricious outburst.

As she sat down on the couch, she and Cole read the statement on the outside: **What, in the world, are you going to do?** They tore into the envelope like five-year-old's opening presents at Christmas. Inside was another card which read: WE NEED TO TALK. SEE YOU SATURDAY, SAME TIME, SAME PLACE!

They met this new communication with both excitement and bewilderment. They were excited to hear from The Teacher again. "I guess this means he's not through with us yet!" Cole exclaimed. "But what in the world does he mean by **What, in the world, are you going to do?** "I wonder if we have gotten off track or if he's upset with the direction we're headed?"

Alisha suggested, "Maybe he needs to get us back on track or something."

Cole replied, "The good news is we only have to wait one day to find out."

Time seemed to stand still for the two of them all day the next day. Excited to see what The Teacher had to tell them they made all the necessary arrangements. They took the kids to grandma's house again. (Thank God for grandmas!) They cleared their calendar of the usual busy stuff they had planned for Saturday. They each went over their actions and reactions over the past several months. They didn't want to get caught unprepared.

With feelings of trepidation, they walked into the coffee shop. It was a little like being called to the principal's office. They were expecting to be chastised for failing to meet expectations.

One look at his face removed all the fear of failure that had, as usual, paralyzed them over the past twenty-four hours. "I am pleased with your effort and focus these past few months," he remarked. "You are making considerable progress in applying the spiritual patterns and principles and the intentional building blocks to your daily lives." Then he added almost with a hint of humor, "A little rough around the edges for you at times but still remarkable progress! Especially you, Cole," he chuckled. Cole responded with a nervous laugh, but without his normal urge to explain or defend himself. He knew that referring to him as rough around the edges was being kind!

W.G. continued his conversation. "Now that you are beginning to experience the results of spending time in the flight simulator and noticing the changes that are taking place in yourselves, I have one question for you." He paused as if expecting them to respond.

"OK," Cole responded. "What is the one question?"

W.G. smiled and replied, "I thought you'd never ask! The one question is, now that you've begun to experience the results of learning and applying the patterns and principles and intentional building blocks in your own lives, **What, in the world, are you going to do?**"

"I'm not sure I follow you," Cole replied. (What a shocker! Who'd of thunk?) "What do you mean, what in the world are we going to do? We are going to continue to spend time in the flight simulator and practice what you've taught us." This time Alisha didn't look at Cole as if he was from Mars; she seemed to share his bewilderment.

"You didn't quite hear the question the way I asked it," the old man replied. "I didn't ask, 'What in the world are you going to do?' What I actually asked was, 'What...*in the world*...are you going to do?' For instance, if you were to discover the cure for cancer, what would you do with that discovery? Would you keep it to yourselves for protection in the event you were to experience the critical disease? Or would you find a way to share it with the world which is being so decimated by it? The world in which you live is being consumed by the disease of broken or unfulfilled relationships. One of every two marriage relationships, in your culture, end in divorce. Sometimes couples who have been married for twenty-plus years find they have 'drifted apart,' I believe is how you explain it. As a matter of fact, that statistic holds true as much for church-going couples as it does for those who do not attend. That breaks my heart! That is not what I mean by abundant living!"

"Now that you have begun to experience the results of applying these spiritual patterns and principles in your own lives, do you plan to keep them to yourselves, 'hid under a bushel' as we say in the business? Will you be content to continue to enjoy the benefits? I know you've begun to experience the need in the lives of some of your friends. This need for changed lives is so great! Will you continue to wait for someone with the need to come to you and beg for the cure? Will you realize the powerful presence that now exists in you that will allow you, if you're willing to obey the call, to pass this relationship-building process on to as many others as possible?"

"What? You mean go and teach others? I'm not sure we can do that. I'm not an eloquent speaker. I don't know what to say. I wouldn't know where to begin," Cole went on with a litany of excuses.

"If I only had a penny for every time I've heard those excuses," W.G. responded. "Eloquence is not required. You don't need to know what to say. I'll help you with that. You begin at the beginning. This doesn't even require you to be smart! This works in your favor, Cole," he chuckled. "It simply requires you to be willing. If you can bring yourself to that point, all the rest will be taken care of."

"We can't be expected to tell others how to do this. We're barely getting the hang of it ourselves. I make more mistakes than successful applications. What will others think? Here I am, 'the screw up,' trying to tell them how to make their lives more meaningful? They will have a field day with me!"

"It seems to me that Ben and Don have already covered that with you. Didn't they tell you that everyone I ever used, down through the ages, was first a 'screw up' before greatness was produced in them? That is the point! If others see that the 'screw up,' as you so aptly put it, can make these changes and produce these results, it must be the result of something or someone other than himself working in his life. If the 'screw-up' can do it, anybody can. *Maybe I can too*, they will think. Then they will begin to **Change the way they think about the things they think about**. That's the multiplication model. You know— Give a man a fish and he'll eat for a day. Teach a man to fish and he'll eat for a lifetime!"

"I still don't get it! What is it that you want us to do, start a class, open a school, write a book? What? Remember, you have to spell it out for me!" Cole began. "Just tell me what you want and I'll do it." The old man glanced at Alisha again with that compassionate look that said, "I know. I've got your back! I'll handle this one."

"It's not about me or anyone else telling you what to do step by step. It's about the journey I want to lead you through to discover how you can join me in my work. An important part of that journey is for you to first discover the many things you SHOULD NOT be doing that get in the way of the few things you SHOULD be doing! Here's your next flight simulator exercise. *Spend some time talking about how*

you understand and utilize TIME. Time is a power-ful concept if you are able to grasp its impact on your life. You admire individuals who seem to be able to get more done than the average person in any given period of time. You think, *They are so lucky! How gifted they are! Or, I could do that too if I had been born with a silver spoon in my mouth!* The secret is not in their giftedness or elevated intelligence or in special opportunities that have been made available to only them. No one, whether prince or pauper, is allotted even one more second than twenty-four hours in any given day. Highly successful people are individuals who understand not just the value of TIME, but the impact of their choice of how to use it. They are able to prioritize, not only the things they are going to commit to doing, but also the things they are going to commit to STOP DOING because of the low level or even negative impact that activity has on their lives.

Remember pattern and principle #12: **Learn to live like you were dying**. Well, you are! You just don't know when that will be. That not knowing should prompt you to make the most of every day as if it would be your last. Over the next few weeks, I want the two of you to spend some time together examining how you use your TIME! For thirty days keep a simple log of how you spend each block of time per day. You may break it up into fifteen-mi-nute segments or one-hour segments. The blocks of time you use are irrelevant. What is relevant is that you make a conscious written note of how you use your TIME. For example, if you spend two hours attending a business meeting, simply write on your log sheet for that day (9–11 a.m. business meeting). Do the same for the many regular activities you engage in each day (i.e., eating, getting showered and dressed in the morning, watching TV, spending time on social media, surfing the web, etc.). At the end of the thirty days see how much time you actually spent in high impact, medium impact, low impact and negative impact activities. After you've completed your audit, start first with making a 'To Stop Doing' list. Then we'll get back together and examine how you've **Changed the way you think** about TIME!"

They left the coffee shop, committed to doing a "Time Audit" for the next thirty days. Cole developed a form they could use with each day of the week for a month broken into thirty-minute segments. They would each keep the printed document in their pocket or purse for ready access. They decided to begin tomorrow. This wouldn't wait until a Monday or the first of the month as they normally would approach a diet or new year's resolution. There seemed to be a different urgency about this endeavor!

About midway through the trial period, they began to notice some unsettling patterns. There seemed to be an awful lot of time eaten up by low impact activity such as TV, web surfing, social media, and just doing nothing. They both concluded that none of these activities were bad in and of themselves. They did, however, realize for the first time how much of their time was consumed by things that had absolutely no positive impact on the quality of their lives. The gold mine in this exercise was the realization that by managing the low and medium impact activities they seemed to have more time each day to do things that had more meaning or a higher impact on their quality of life. They agreed early on in the process not to continue the "TIME AUDIT" but to begin to set a "TIME BUDGET." They made a list of the low impact items and set an allotted amount of time each day or week to spend on them. Writing down this "TIME BUDGET" would help them in prioritizing their activities. They soon realized they slipped up fairly often and fell back into the rut of low impact time usage. But, by the same token, they realized how quickly they were able to help each other catch themselves and begin to hold each other accountable for their use of TIME. They were shocked by the difference this made in what they were able to get done. They began to feel more energized, even at the end of a rigorous day.

They couldn't wait to tell The Teacher.

One afternoon, as they were heading out to dinner for another conversation about their newfound discovery, they noticed a run-down rattle trap of an automobile chugging along ahead of them. After casting a few aspersions on the occupant and his jalopy, Cole pulled up beside him at the traffic light. Looking over with a sympathetic (and highly condescending) expression, he was flabbergasted to see— yep—The Teacher grinning like a "possum eating chitlins!" He smiled and signaled for them to pull over. Cole looked for a place to get out of traffic, and just ahead was an empty parking place. He pulled into the parking spot only to realize they were sitting directly in front of the coffee shop. They looked at each other as if to say, "That never happens! We never get a parking spot right in front! But then, what do you expect when dealing with W.G.?"

"Well, how is it going?" the old man said. "That's a rhetorical question isn't it," chided Cole. "You know full well how it's going. That's why you're here and how we got a parking place right in front!" This time it was The Teacher replying, "Busted! You got me!" They all had a good laugh.

"Well," he continued. "Now that you have discovered both the value and impact of TIME **What, in the world, are you going to do?** He looked at Cole as if he was fully expecting him to rattle off a list of frustrations and objections but with a calming expression on his face.

"We have been giving some thought to that question since you first brought it up," Cole began. "Alisha and I have both encountered a few opportunities to share what you've taught us with our friends. We decided that teaching a class on the patterns and principles and building blocks would not be productive. That approach is an academic exercise and they are skills-based learning. So, we've begun a discussion group to discuss the spiritual patterns and principles and intentional building blocks with several couples who have expressed an interest. A couple of them have even brought friends and family members to join in the discussion. We talk about each item and then create among the group a 'flight simulator' exercise to allow us to practice what we talked about each week. The following week, we begin with a discussion about how the previous week went and what worked and didn't work so well. I have given some thought to what we can do beyond that," he said. Then he paused and gave The Teacher a glance, looking for approval which he promptly received by way of a smile, a nod, and a noticeable gleam in his eye that said, "I'm listening!"

Cole continued, "I have realized that this is a process that will require us to be proactive and not merely reactive. We can't wait for people to come to us, but we must go out to where they are to share what you've taught us. So, I've created a website to help others to begin to approach that 'Next-Level Living' that everyone talks about but never seems to be able to reach. It contains information about groups that are pursuing being more intentional in their lives. It also has a blog which allows us to share and discuss the patterns and principles and the intentional building blocks with people we don't even know and may never meet. It opens up a whole new world to allow you to reach out and touch lives through us that we never before thought possible. I've begun to get hits from all around the world asking about the process, the patterns and principles, and the building blocks. I've even had some suggestions that I write a book to share your life-changing patterns and principles. I've never considered myself to be 'a writer' but I have begun the process. Heaven only knows where that will go!" he concluded, and then realizing what he had just said he added, sheepishly, "But I guess you already knew that!" They all got a chuckle out of that.

W.G. responded with a smile and glowing look on his face. "I am pleased that you are beginning to realize that this is not dependent on your talent, intelligence, or even your position in society. I want you to continue to step out in faith knowing that, as long as you 'SEEK' me I will be available and I will bless the work you do on behalf of others with passion and without regard to what you will receive in return. I promise you will not be disappointed but greatly blessed by giving selflessly of your time, your talents, your energy, and your resources. I will always be with you. I will never leave you. Even when you can't visibly see me, rest assured, in good times and bad, I am there." As The Teacher left, he also handed them an envelope. Inside was another single sheet of parchment paper and a business card. The card read:

> *W.G. Atap (With God All Things Are Possible)*
>
> *I Am, I Just Am! When you 'SEEK' me, I will be found.*
>
> *I am with you always. I will never leave you.*

The parchment paper, also in the beautiful print read:

> **The building blocks for an intentional marriage relationship:**
>
> 1. **Understanding, Respect, and Trust** (that's one, not three!).
>
> 2. **Communication** comes in three styles: Casual, Conflict and Committed.
>
> 3. **Responsibility**: to and for self and to and for each other.
>
> 4. **Accountability**: to self and to each other.
>
> 5. **Action**: the results you desire come from right actions, not right ideas.

As they left the coffee shop and headed for home, Cole and Alisha, for the first time since meeting Ben and Don and The Teacher, felt OK with his disappearance from their sight. They realized He is still with them, just not in a physically visible way. They finally realized what He meant when He said, "Wherever two or more are gathered in my name, there will I be also." They had a newfound peace about them and a sense of direction and excitement about what the future held for them and those with whom they would come in contact.

In their next life planning review and evaluation, they did some work on their life's mission statement. After much discussion and many attempts, they finally adopted "To help others reach their full God-given potential" as their mission statement and a motto that read, "Just Good is just not good enough."

9 780578 886749